Journalist and author **Vanessa Holburn** spent two years campaigning
fo ban on third-party pet sales in a bid to end the cruel practice of
pu py farming. In 2018, she was invited to Downing Street to hear
M hael Gove announce plans to change the law to support such a
ba The campaign is proof that ordinary people together can achieve
ex aordinary change.

Her current focus is 'greening' her small Berkshire village –
ac ising business and community groups how to use and waste less
an move towards becoming plastic-free, while sharing skills and
re urces.

Vanessa's publishing experience stretches over 24 years and
he work has appeared in magazines, newspapers and digital
ou ets. Her consumer press credits include *Private Eye*, the *Mirror*,
th *Sun, Vegan Living, Woman's Own, Yours, Dogs Today, Ask the
Do tor* and the *Independent on Sunday*.

Praise for *How to Be an Activist*

'I wish this book had been available when I started campaigning. It's everything you need to know to get you through some of the most intense, and ultimately most rewarding, acts of your life'
Sarah Brisdion, campaigner for accessible toilets (Changing Places)

'We all have an inner activist and, with world leaders largely refusing to properly engage on everything from climate change to mental health, there's never been a more important time to harness her. This book allows you to learn from the experiences of trail-blazing campaigners and make your own positive difference'
Natasha Devon MBE, activist and author of
A Beginner's Guide to Being Mental

'Activism isn't just a hobby, it's a fun and exciting lifestyle'
Hugo Sugg, Campaign Director Hugo's Earthquake

'Despite the Brexit chaos, politicians made time for Lucy's Law because it reminded them why they wanted to be MPs. Passionate individuals highlighted something that was broken they could fix. If you want a better future, please read this book and find your voice!'
Beverley Cuddy, Editor of *Dogs Today* and Publisher of *Dogs Monthly*

'Practical, persuasive and personal, this is important reading for grassroots campaigners. It will be of interest to anyone impelled to take matters into their own hands, when the failures of those who are meant to act on our behalves in times of crisis fail us'

Mike Schwarz, civil liberties lawyer

'There's no time like the present to try and help make the world a kinder and safer place for all beings. This wonderful book will empower you to get up off your sofa and make that change'

Emily Lawrence, wildlife campaigner

'*How To Be An Activist* is a fantastic book, bringing people from all walks of life into politics to ensure that citizens' campaigns thrive'

Dr Lisa Cameron MP

'Never before has activism been so accessible or aspirational, and Vanessa's book makes a dream to make a difference a real possibility. This easy-to-read, simple-to-digest guide not only explains how to bring people together and make a difference, but, with case studies and takeaways, *How to Be An Activist* provides guidance for anyone who wants to be the difference this world needs right now'

Natalie Trice, PR Director and charity founder

How to Be an Activist

A practical guide to organising,
campaigning and making change happen

••••••••••••••

Vanessa Holburn

A How To Book

ROBINSON

ROBINSON

First published in Great Britain in 2020
by Robinson

10 9 8 7 6 5 4 3 2 1

A CIP catalogue record for this book
is available from the British Library.

ISBN: 978-1-47214-384-6

Typeset in Great Britain by
Mousemat Design Limited

Printed and bound in Great Britain by
Clays Ltd, Elcograf S.p.A.

Papers used by Robinson are from well-
managed forests and other sustainable
sources

Robinson
An imprint of
Little, Brown Book Group
Carmelite House
50 Victoria Embankment
London EC4Y 0DZ

An Hachette UK Company
www.hachette.co.uk

www.littlebrown.co.uk

How To Books are published by
Robinson, an imprint of Little,
Brown Book Group. We welcome
proposals from authors who have
first-hand experience of their
subjects. Please set out the aims of
your book, its target market and its
suggested contents in an email to
howto@littlebrown.co.uk

To all those that I stood alongside –
and especially Marc Abraham for leading
the #LucysLaw campaign

Contents

Foreword

by **Lorraine Platt**

Co-Founder, Conservative Animal Welfare Foundation
Co-Founder, Conservatives Against Fox Hunting
Founder, Blue Badger
Founder, Blue Hare
Board Member, Save the Asian Elephants
IFAW Campaigner Award 2012
RSPCA Lord Erskine Award 2014
Inspirations Awards for Women Finalist 2013
CEVA Animal Welfare Finalist Award 2016

'Never doubt that a small group of thoughtful, committed citizens can change the world; indeed, it's the only thing that ever has.'

Margaret Mead

Grassroots campaigns are about bringing people together to make inspirational change happen; to engage like-minded individuals with your cause and create action that helps transform any perceived conceptions and enables the change to take place that brings about the objective of your campaign. That might sound like a huge mountain to climb – however, Vanessa Holburn has written the perfect step-by-step guide to help you reach the summit of your goals and achieve your aim.

It is a well-known saying that change starts with someone somewhere taking that first single step. Often it is into the unknown and the path ahead may be strewn with obstructions and cliff edges. It may feel like walking a tightrope at times, especially if the issue is sensitive or controversial. Vanessa's book helps guide you and prepares the campaigner for all eventualities.

'Walking the talk' is paramount, and sustainable action requires planning, dedication, commitment, consistency and discipline. It's important to define your goals and just how they can be achieved from the onset in order to be most effective and avoid wasting precious energy. It could be something as simple as a petition, for example, to help flag up support to 'end live exports' and deliver it to the decision-makers responsible for legislation. Be clear in your mind about what defines your success; your message needs to be clear and it needs to make a powerful impact to the right audience. It also needs to appeal to them in a way that makes them ready to engage with the campaign. Vanessa, with clear examples, shows how individuals have taken their own campaigns and grown them from the seeds of an idea to successful national movements.

Some public activism involves peaceful family marches while others may be loud, noisy, vocal protests and may not appeal to all of us. We all have a choice about how to use our voice, when to play our part or demur to participate and find another way to make our message heard.

There is no absolute successful campaign template today; social media enables us to create an effective movement that would have been beyond contemplation before its availability. The Internet provides us with abundant resources and enables us to interact with key stakeholders from almost the beginning of our campaigns. You will find opposition, you may even face ridicule, but remember – this is your dream, your campaign, and you want to change the world and make a positive difference.

Don't worry about your campaign not being perfect – just do it. It will evolve organically, and opportunities will happen. Achieving something imperfectly is better than aiming for perfection and achieving nothing at all. Authenticity is special and people will connect with this. Heart will tell the story that needs to be told – go for it and seize the day!

Keep burn-out at bay by being kind to yourself with a short switch-off now and then with time completely away from campaigning and relaxing with family and friends. As often as you can, surround yourself with supportive people and ignore negative critics who don't support your campaign. Save your valuable energy for those who can contribute towards achieving your goal and make the campaign a success.

There comes a time for the talking to stop – this book is all about people taking action. So get up, get going, blaze a trail and make change happen – it's time for people power!

Introduction

What is your passion?

Have you ever felt so unhappy and frustrated about something, you wanted to change it? The amount of unnecessary packaging used on fruit and veg in supermarkets; the gender pay gap; or the low-welfare farming of puppies for profit, for example? Well, you and me both. And my desire to stop the practice of selling 'throwaway' pets in third-party retail environments opened my eyes to a whole new way to turn my passion into action. And I want to share the lessons I've learned along the way with you.

In 2018, activism in the UK by ordinary citizens led to one of the biggest examples of peaceful civil disobedience in decades, as thousands of people gathered on five London bridges to protest climate breakdown and species extinction. That July, campaigners raised almost £18,000 to pay for a comic inflatable blimp to show their dissatisfaction with a visit to the UK by US President Donald Trump. The capital also played host to massive marches by those demanding a second referendum on Brexit and gender equality.

By 2019, the public's taste for activism grew. In February, more than sixty towns and cities around the country saw school pupils walk out to attend protests that called on the Government to declare a climate emergency and take active steps to tackle the problem. An estimated 15,000 people took part.

Just a month later, after Theresa May's Brexit deal was rejected time and time again in Parliament – even by her own MPs – it was reported that over one million people joined an anti-Brexit march in London. At the same time, a petition on the Parliament website asking for Article 50 to be revoked garnered more than six million signatures and crashed the site due to the unprecedented take-up.

By April 2019, the capital saw a wave of protests organised by Extinction Rebellion, who occupied four sites across London, blocked roads, disrupted train travel and protested at Heathrow Airport. More than a thousand activists were arrested following the campaign but the media reported that the public widely supported the protests[1].

In February 2019, YouGov released a poll that showed 82 per cent of Britons thought that 'politics is broken'. It seems our nation had woken up – and everyday people have become disenchanted with democracy and want to make a change. Perhaps you are one of them?

But turning your discontent into a practical and successful campaign that makes a difference is no easy feat. You'll need clear objectives, armfuls of information and a dedicated and co-operative team. Which is where this book comes in – it's a practical guide that explains how to identify what you want to achieve and how to go about doing it. Read on if you want to make a difference through activism!

What do you want to change?

The first question you need to ask yourself is: why have you chosen this book? What is the change you want to make? Perhaps an issue has affected someone you love – a friend or a family member? Or your focus may be far wider than that – a problem that touches the whole of society that you want to help solve? This book will help you identify what you want to achieve and how to plan for success. It offers a step-by-step guide for accessing the necessary information and support, organising a campaign and getting your message out there. Along the way, you'll gain insights from some

---

[1] https://www.theguardian.com/environment/2019/apr/24/support-for-extinction-rebellion-soars-in-wake-of-easter-protests

other great campaigners and activists who have been exactly where you are today.

A happy side-effect

Be warned: activism is rewarding – and it is rather addictive! I've made new friends, gained an understanding of how local and national government works and stepped away from being politically apathetic. While writing this book, I have realised just how much I've learned and developed over the last few years of campaigning. For many, activism is cathartic and helps achieve what the experts call 'post-traumatic growth', the idea that there can be positive psychological effects and a new sense of personal strength following stressful or traumatic events – 'what doesn't kill you makes you stronger'. This is particularly true for those who have suffered personally or watched someone they love suffer. Often, the tougher the circumstances, the more inner strength is uncovered. Activism can push you to your limits, help you find new skills and abilities and force you to acquire knowledge.

What will success look like?

An often-overlooked aspect of activism is the setting of milestones and goals, so you know exactly what you have achieved. Believe me, it's essential for morale that you see your time and energy expenditure as worthwhile. This guide will help you to outline an end point for your campaign, too, as well as celebrate all the small wins in between. It will encourage you to silence that inner critic and to recognise when it's time to put away the placard and toast your success.

So, let's get active ...

Part I

Getting Started

Why Individual Activism?

What exactly is activism?

The dictionary definition of activism is 'the policy or action of using vigorous campaigning to bring about political or social change', but perhaps a simpler way to think of activism is to see it as the process of taking part in one or more of a wide range of activities that challenge the status quo. These activities can be anything from grand public gestures such as gluing your hands to a government building to small personal changes like taking a reusable cup to your preferred coffee shop every day and actively encouraging others to do the same.

Typically, the mention of activism conjures up visions of direct action such as protests, strikes and other public demonstrations. But, in reality, activism is just as likely to involve raising awareness and providing education, perhaps in schools and workplaces or on the street, or by charting your progress in a blog to inspire others. It involves fundraising; taking responsibility for an individual project or programme that tackles a specific social problem, like the setting up of a food bank or a period-poverty scheme; or changing your own lifestyle to reflect your ideals.

Both individuals and groups use activism, with the ultimate aim of bringing more and more support to the cause until the policy-makers responsible for the issue notice, listen and make change. Without activism, the UK would still be farming fur, there would be no child sex-offender disclosure scheme (dubbed Sarah's Law) and women wouldn't be able to vote or access birth control. It's hard to imagine our world without activism.

Are you an 'activist'?

By default, an activist is a person who campaigns to bring about political or social change, but for many it's quite a step to consider themselves as an activist. This is because the person on the street may hold negative associations about the term, thinking of an activist as eccentric, militant, or sometimes even aggressive. Of course, extreme and unorthodox acts of activism attract the most attention – particularly in the press – but law-abiding and gentle citizens who work tirelessly on campaigns for years on end bring about just as much progress.

There was nothing outlandish about holding a free 5km run in a public park where everyone and anyone was welcome to take part, but now the self-organised Parkrun is a global phenomenon, bringing communities together and improving health across generations and social divides. It has helped to establish that running is free for everyone regardless of fitness level. Imagine the lives it has changed, and the friendships and communities it has built.

You might also feel that you are too insignificant or unimportant to make a difference as an activist and later in the book we'll discuss the inner critic and imposter syndrome many face as they work towards change. In reality, anyone who tries to make a difference for the good of others – yes, even you! – is in effect an activist, although they might be happier to use the less pejorative terms 'campaigner' or 'advocate'.

And you should never underestimate the power of the individual campaigner or activist or of casting yourself in that role. Even The Body Shop founder Anita Roddick started modestly; Roddick admitted that the idea to recycle the product bottles was borne out of necessity rather than concerns for the environment! Interestingly, in 2019, The Body Shop announced it was planning to turn its shops into 'activist hubs' to encourage campaigning and localised activism. The move represents a return to examining its original brand positioning – The Body Shop was a key part of the campaigning team that lobbied the EU for the ban on animal-tested cosmetics that came into force in 2013.

So, are you an activist? If you've chosen this book because you want to make a change locally, nationally or globally, then it's likely that if you're not one already, you're about to become an activist. Welcome to the club – you're not alone!

The age of activism

It's fair to say that the UK population – from schoolchildren to pensioners – has become increasingly frustrated with the culture of the professional politician and mainstream policies. All too often, those in charge of the established political parties seem more interested in leadership coups, establishing their own larger-than-life personalities and scoring points in the House than responding to the day-to-day issues that affect and motivate the voting public.

Meanwhile, access to NHS treatment varies widely across the country, there's a funding crisis in our schools and extremist parties are forming at both ends of the political spectrum. When David Cameron confidently called a referendum in June 2016 on EU membership and the public voted, it was the first time a UK-wide referendum result had gone against the preferred choice of the Government. Shocked by the result and his massive misjudgement, he quickly stepped aside.

Within a few years, Brexit negotiations were stalled, senior politicians had begun to leave their parties to join what became the Independent Group For Change (which, in turn, suffered its own problems) and MPs took over the Commons agenda. From the pages of the *Guardian*, Michael Heseltine called Brexit the 'biggest peacetime crisis we have faced' and said that a no-deal Brexit could 'provoke a national emergency'.

And since the start of the Brexit turmoil, there seems to be an increasing appetite among the British public for getting out there to 'be the change you want to see' as the saying goes. Ordinary people are getting involved in projects such as community orchards, marches to protect our wildlife and hashtag campaigns such as #NotGuilty, which works to combat sexual violence and misdirected victim blame. Celebrities like Chris Packham and Stephen Fry are the latest in a long list of household names happy to use their fame to attract attention to their causes; and anti-fracking protestors have even proved they are prepared to go to jail to get their message across.

Welcome to the age of activism! But what happens next?

Case Study – the First-Time Activists

Jo, 45, from Hampshire, attended both of the #PeoplesVote marches that took place in London in 2018. They are the only political marches she has ever taken part in. She says, 'I don't think I've ever felt as strongly about anything before. I feel this is really affecting me personally. I feel like I just can't sit back and accept it. I also feel like none of the political parties are representing my point of view, so I need to do something to make my voice heard.'

Caroline, 46, divides her time between Surrey and Paris. She attended the #RiseForClimate march in Paris in September 2018, describing it as 'the most amazing day – thousands of people coming together to protest peacefully about probably the biggest issue facing our planet today'. Feeling that governments are not listening to the irrefutable evidence for global warming, and that things are reaching critical point, she explains, 'Rather than just feeling frustrated about it all, I felt compelled to do something positive. Taking to the streets felt very empowering and, as it was one of many similar events around the world, I like to hope that together we made a difference.' She also feels it is now our 'personal duty' to do something, and that 'the time has come to take things to the next level'.

Sam, from London, is in his first year of secondary school and is one of a group of friends who missed school to attend the 2019 climate-change march in London. It was the first time he had been on a demo. He says, 'By going to the protest, I hope to get my voice heard and hope that they make new laws about climate change.'

Juliette, 44, from Berkshire, also attended the two 2018 marches to protest against Brexit and plans to attend more. She says, 'I've never been on a march before but I felt compelled to go. Brexit stirred something in me. I have always felt European and now, suddenly, I'm told I'm not. By going along I felt I was marching for my children's futures, which I firmly believe lie in our union with the EU and all the freedoms this brings.'

Anna, 38, from South Devon, attended the 2019 global school strike for climate-change march, and took her seven-year-old daughter out of school to attend (with authorisation from the head teacher). In the past, Ann admits she has viewed protests and marches as scary and confrontational, but the child-led nature of this one meant she did not feel intimidated. She explains her motives for attending: 'I feel compelled to speak up – time is running out before climate change becomes irreversible and we can no longer slow it down, but governments are not doing anything about it. I also believe in the power of the youth voice – a child's protest is pure and honest and without ulterior motive ... you can't really argue with that.'

She adds, 'I couldn't just sit by and watch – I feel that this time I am part of the change, whereas previously I maybe haven't been as engaged or as politically aware and not felt empowered or driven to stand up for what I believe in.' She wants to teach her daughter 'that it's important to stand up for what we believe in'.

Takeaways

- First-time activists come in all guises – they can be young or old, and everything in between
- Today's political climate has resulted in an increased taste for activism
- Many of those who take up campaigning feel 'compelled' to do so – they are passionate about the central issue/s
- It's never the wrong time to become a change maker!

2

Identifying the Problem

What do you want to change?
The first step in making meaningful change is to decide exactly what you want to achieve and why. And while this might sound simple at first, it requires a full understanding of the issue at hand and an analysis of what needs to be different to allow permanent change to happen. This will allow you to decide who or what to target in order to achieve your goal.

For example, when I first stood outside a garden centre protesting about the sale of puppies there, I was unaware of how my local council's licensing department and outdated animal welfare laws were conspiring to enable this abhorrent practice. And while I knew instinctively that an ethical dog breeder would never want or need to sell their puppies in this manner, I had little idea of the scale of the puppy farming industry both here and overseas, and the money that could be made through low-welfare, high-volume dog breeding. And little did I realise the co-dependence of one upon the other.

I also failed to understand how buying a pet in a retail environment – not unlike one where you might pick out the latest 'on-trend' handbag – was acceptable to so many consumers. For me, it was intuitive that purchasing a pet would be a responsible decision taken only after careful deliberation, and that it was unacceptable to keep puppies caged on a shop floor. But for many others, this was how they viewed a pet – as a commodity to be bought and sold without too much awareness or concern about its provenance. I had much to learn about the puppy trade itself and the people at both ends of the chain.

Ask yourself these questions

As I outlined above, the issues that both allowed and encouraged the sale of pets in places such as shops, garden centres, boot fairs and online via sites such as Gumtree were more complex than I first realised. And I had to educate myself as to why such places existed, why they were thriving and why people were prepared to buy in this manner at all.

The answers in this case were that the practice (perhaps unbelievably) was perfectly legal; local councils were given free reign to inspect, license and regulate retail outlets (despite being unlikely to possess relevant specialist knowledge) and the buying public lacked the information or concern it needed to realise that such places are simply the well-dressed windows of animal abuse on a massive scale. Only by thoroughly understanding the forces at play here and the relationship between them could my fellow campaigners and I really work to stop the practice for good.

Just like me, you will need to ask what laws, regulations, practices, behaviours and beliefs are allowing what you want to change to persist, unchecked. Will you need to tackle the local council or the Government? Is there a regulatory or industry body you might petition? Is it a matter that Trading Standards should be dealing with? Do the general public or a specific section of the community need educating? Who can be held accountable for a practice or activity you want to change? Do you need to change laws or perceptions, or perhaps both? Is the problem local, national or global?

Each answer will ultimately help you understand what you need to focus on to facilitate change – and how you should plan your campaign. Armed with this knowledge, you can understand your core aims, the messages you need to communicate and to whom they must be delivered.

Checklist

Ask yourself:
- What do you want to achieve? A change in law and/or regulations – or a change in beliefs and behaviour?
- What must change?
- How can change be effected? By a ban or better education, for example?
- Who must you target to bring change (maybe there is more than one person)?
- Who can you hold to account?
- Do the general public need education?
- What is your central message?

Who will it help?

A further consideration is: who will benefit from any changes you make? It might be the general public, local residents, parents, the disabled or perhaps the users of a local or national service. It could be a specific age, ethnicity, gender or sexual orientation demographic. It could also be a combination of these. In my case, the breeding bitches trapped in puppy farms and their traumatised offspring were the immediate and obvious winners. However, the puppy-buying consumer also had a lot to gain because farmed pets often come with expensive and stress-inducing long-term health and psychological problems alongside infectious diseases, which may also require immediate and costly vet treatment. Some might even die shortly after purchase causing heartbreak to the unprepared new owners, who may have bought the puppy as a family pet, thereby unwittingly causing distress to their children.

Whatever the case, these beneficiaries are the people who will become your allies and your greatest supporters. They know why things must change and the problems that will arise if things remain the same because they have first-hand experience of the problem. They can provide the anecdotal and physical evidence you need to take your case to the authorities. They are the 'face' of the story that will capture the attention of the press and the wider audience. Their ongoing support will lift you to success.

Conversely, those who might lose out financially, socially or in some other way – whether that is a perceived or real loss – when you succeed, will become your biggest detractors. But don't worry – how to deal with your critics effectively will be covered in Chapter 19.

What would be an ideal end point?

Alongside setting specific goals that you want to achieve and identifying targets for your message, another crucial aspect of planning an active campaign to bring about change is to consider your end point. Ask yourself what constitutes success in this campaign – is it a new law, improved regulations, a conviction, an appeal, a review or investigation or raising awareness and changing attitudes? Sometimes, it might even be a combination of these things.

While it's important to recognise little victories along the way (more about this later), when you've decided what qualifies as success, you will use that to work out a battle plan.

Case Study – Natasha Devon MBE

Natasha tours UK schools and colleges delivering talks and conducting research on mental health, body image, gender and social equality. She's responsible for the *Mental Health Media Charter* (*MHMC*) and the 'Where's Your Head At?' campaign, which calls for a change in the law to protect the mental health of British workers.

'I recovered from an eating disorder in 2006 and had this embryonic notion about doing something in schools,' explains Natasha, knowing that the mental-health education she'd received had had little effect. So she visited schools and asked 500 teenagers what their concerns were. When body image consistently ranked highly, she created a suitable education programme, working with the charity Body Gossip. She continues this successful and intuitive formula today, asking young people what they want and then providing it.

For Natasha, working predominantly with 13-18-year-olds is an essential part of her strategy. She describes teens as ' brilliant people', 'smart enough to understand how the world works, but still at a point in their lives where their ideas are fluid enough to be challenged'. And because of her longstanding and regular work in schools, she's now invited to various health and education select committees to report on any trends she is seeing; this helps to inform effective solutions, and so enables real change.

While education is a crucial part of Natasha's work, alongside visiting schools she campaigns to change the system and environment for young people. Natasha is the author of the *Mental Health Media Charter*, a set of seven simple guidelines for ensuring imagery and language used in mental-health reporting is responsible, educational and stigma-reducing. She deliberately designed transparent and accessible recommendations, working on them with mental-health organisations and those with first-hand experience of mental illness. Launched on World Mental Health Day in October 2017, Natasha asked the media and influencers to sign up to the charter – over a hundred have, including *Grazia* and *Heat* magazines and the *Times Educational Supplement*. She also asks the public to 'vote with their feet', boycotting outlets that do not adopt the charter.

Natasha is also trying to change workplace law, making it compulsory for businesses to ensure there are mental-health first-aiders for their employees. A Change.org petition triggered a debate in the House of Commons in January 2019; a cross-party group of MPs overwhelmingly backed the motion to update the Health and Safety at Work Act to ensure mental health is treated equally to physical health in the workplace. While this success won't automatically lead to a new law, Natasha will continue to lobby until the changes are made.

Success is all about teamwork for Natasha, who works with a couple of mental-health charities in a 'two-way process', sharing her findings from schools and, in turn, accessing the charity's robust research to inform her work. 'Campaigning is best when it's a joint effort,' she adds, 'because charities are often restricted in what they are allowed to say publicly, but will more than happily lend their research to outspoken activists like me to highlight important topics.'

Her advice to would-be activists is to 'just do it – and then follow it through!' And don't worry if your idea isn't perfect, she says, 'You can evolve your project down the line but get your webpage up, copyright your campaign name and start drumming up support/discussion as soon as you can ... Remember, the average person doesn't care about the issue as much as you do. People also need to hear about a person or project a minimum of seven times before they'll remember it. So keep plugging away.'

Takeaways

- Do you have personal experiences you could share to make your campaign personal and informed?
- What barriers to change are you aware of? Work out how you can tackle them.
- Who could you work with to achieve your goals? Is there an NGO involved in the issue that could provide help and support?
- Can you summarise your aims succinctly?
- Don't procrastinate – get out there and make a start (and figure the rest out along the way!)

Finding Your Tribe

Why do you need to find a team?

When poet John Donne wrote 'no man is an island', he neatly summed up the age-old realisation that humans thrive when they work together within a community and do not fare as well if they try to go it alone. This is especially true within the arena of campaigning and every activist should seek out a team of like-minded individuals to work with and rely upon as they achieve their shared goals.

On a practical level, other people can bring skills and knowledge to the campaign that you may not possess. For example, they might offer valuable experience that their day job affords them – such as knowledge of the legal, fundraising, financial, marketing, data protection, PR or press industries – each of which could become essential during your work. They may have a knack for research and investigative work, a flair for public speaking, an encyclopaedic knowledge of facts and figures, a photographic memory, or an amazing ability to network and make friends. Are they the queen of catchy slogans or an ace photographer? Perhaps they'll bring with them some useful contacts or the ability to motivate the masses for a march. Maybe they have access to printing facilities or other resources that will save you money? Certain people also offer boundless enthusiasm that is as infectious as it is welcome, or can bring their time and financial backing to a project.

Every skill, talent, characteristic and attribute will come into its own as your campaign progresses. You should always be ready to accept the help that your campaign team and wider supporters offer, even if you're more used to being self-reliant.

Specialist skills

It's likely that people who are attracted to a specific cause will already have relevant specialist knowledge, too. This was the case with our grassroots campaign to ask Wokingham Borough Council to stop licensing the sale of puppies from a garden centre, which quickly attracted the attention of those with veterinary and canine behavioural backgrounds. Those working with animals locally had direct experience with puppies and dogs that had suffered because of where they came from and how they had been sold. And when you can speak with authority and experience, an audience will be inclined to listen. You'll also be ready for any questions that are thrown your way by members of the public, local and national government officials, lawmakers and the media.

You will also benefit from connecting with people who already have campaigning experience. This could include people who are fighting for the same cause in another area or at a different level, who are active in similar issues or activists who lobby on a different matter but use similar methods. Experienced campaigners have trodden this path before and know what works and what doesn't. They'll be able to share their knowledge – from making effective protest banners and telling you how to prepare a petition for maximum impact and engagement to which MPs and pressure groups can offer help and support.

Every single person that comes to the group brings with them a different skillset that can become invaluable as your campaign develops. And despite being united by their common aim, they typically also have the benefit of coming from a wide spectrum of backgrounds which offers a diversity that pays dividends in both widening your reach and communicating your message.

Emotional support

Let's not forget that holding an opinion that differs from others – or wanting to go that bit further and make a positive change – can be a lonely experience. You might find friends and/or family do not share your concerns – or even understand exactly what the issue is that you feel so passionate about. Those you have some things in common with – because you work together, attended school together, live close by, share children of the same age or enjoy a similar leisure activity – may not sympathise with your other beliefs. They might consider traditional methods of activism extreme or even dangerous. Here, once again, your campaign team can save you from feeling marooned on that island Donne referred to.

A team of activists can help each other through the tougher times – when your cause seems unimportant and derailed by others, for example. A campaign team will give each other courage and confidence, and celebrate every small achievement, giving credit where it is due, and allow everyone the opportunity to contribute. When you work for a common cause, these people become your tribe, your squad – and you are brought closer because your core beliefs and moral compass bind you together despite differences in age, gender, lifestyle and background. Which is just as well, because you'll likely be seeing them more and more as you work through your campaign!

How to find like-minded individuals

But where do you recruit your team? Well, social media is a great place to make new friends and supporters – and it's free! You can search out and find groups, pages, posts, people and hashtags across Twitter, Facebook, Instagram, LinkedIn and YouTube that are working towards similar goals. Become involved and interact with comments and posts, and see where your aims overlap. If your cause is one involving animal welfare, for example, it's likely vegan and cruelty-free groups and individuals would be interested, too. Be bold and make yourself known – you have nothing to lose. If you can't find anything on social media that seems to represent your cause already, create and promote it, and invite others to join.

An open Facebook group or page is a particularly good way to gather supporters together and encourage engagement. As well as posting your own comments, you can keep everyone updated with the issue when it appears in the media and with similar activities and campaigns to yours. People who want to become more involved in your work are able to message you, too. The Facebook tips section can advise if setting up a group or page suits your needs better, but here are a few of the major differences:

Facebook Pages
- Visible to everyone on the Internet by default
- Offer an authentic and public presence on Facebook for public figures, businesses and organisations
- Facebook verifies pages for authenticity

Facebook Groups
- You can decide if your Group is public, or if members require approval to join, or if it is by invitation only
- Designed for small groups to communicate, share their common interests and opinions
- Can be anything from a sports team to political commentary

Another great way to reach out to people online is by creating an online petition or fundraiser. Both of these options allow you to interact with your supporters and post updates. I discuss these topics more fully in Chapters 9 and 15.

Alternatively, consider building an informative website using one of the free online platforms such as Wix or Weebly, or blogger platforms such as WordPress and Blogger. A website will give you the ability to compose a simple explanation of the problem and possible solutions, as well as enabling you to publicise events and offer contact details to those wanting to become involved.

Before there was Google!

Of course, long before the age of the YouTube influencer or Instagram star, there were other ways to 'make friends and influence people', and these traditional methods of communication, such as face-to-face contact, are still viable. These approaches will also capture an audience that does not engage with the Internet that often, or even at all. Such activities offer a chance to disseminate information, offer advice and collect both signatures for a petition and donations for the cause. If your issue is a particularly local one, outreach may also uncover those personally affected by it who may not have otherwise come across.

Consider setting up a stand in your local area – perhaps in a busy shopping thoroughfare – or maybe at an event where many people might be interested. For us, a local fun dog show provided a chance to educate people about the provenance of pet shop pups and make contact with people who shared our goals. If your campaign is focused on a topic that centres on funding for education or healthcare, schools, colleges and hospitals might be a suitable location. Bear in mind, however, that you may need to ask permission to stand on privately owned or council land.

Marches, vigils and demonstrations are also a way to meet more potential supporters and it's worth carrying take-away information when you organise and attend these events. And if you are planning a protest in a public forum it's always worth seeing if you can encourage the local and national press to come along. Every piece of coverage is an opportunity to drum up more support. Typically, the media love a good turnout for a photo op – and people also love to see themselves in the paper or on TV, too – so it's a win-win!

Finally, remember to appoint a person or several people and use a shared email address or a mobile number to speak to anyone who wishes to learn more or contact you after the event. Try to agree on several simple points that you'd like to communicate to anyone who asks questions, so that your message is clear and consistent. It's also important that what you say to casual enquirers is correct and not likely to cause the campaign to be accused of slander or defamation. Some members of the team may be more suited to this role than others.

Like-minded and umbrella organisations

It's unlikely that you are the only person affected by the issue you are campaigning on or about. It might be a local concern linked to a national or even global one, or a topic that concerns individuals across the world irrespective of class, gender and culture. Because of this, it's likely that somewhere else there exists a group of activists not unlike yourselves, and perhaps a larger central organisation taking a wider view on things. Other groups that share the same or similar goals to you can be a goldmine of support and information. They can also help to swell your campaign numbers and allow you to see the bigger picture. A quick search online will bring up groups and individuals you could reach out to.

Some organisations to consider:

- Citizens UK
- Feminist and Women's Studies Association
- Global Justice Now
- Human Rights Watch
- League Against Cruel Sports
- Stonewall
- Sustain

Be aware of data protection

As you go about your advocacy role, be aware that in the UK the law rigorously protects the collection and storage of the details of any of your supporters – essentially 'personal information' – even when that information is given freely to you. This means that if you have any kind of database to help you connect and contact those people who are interested in hearing more from you, you must be fully compliant with the Data Protection Act 2018, which you'll also hear referred to as 'the General Data Protection Regulation (GDPR)'.

The current GDPR regulations came into force in May 2018 and cover any piece of information that can be used to identify a person – typically their name and address, for example – but also data such as an IP address. One of the most important aspects of the law is that individuals must give consent for their details to be stored – in theory, this could even mean if they are scribbled on a handwritten petition. I'd recommend that anyone who could be considered to be collecting personal details covers the basics. This includes:

- Obtaining consent
- Having a data protection policy in place, with a statement about how data is processed and that data held will be destroyed after a certain period of time has elapsed (possibly several years)
- Providing a secure location for data storage

The new regulations came about after several high-profile cases of data leaks by the likes of Yahoo and LinkedIn and are enforced by the Information Commissioner's Office (ICO). While your campaign may be relatively small-scale compared to that, the ICO can instigate criminal investigations and issue fines, so even volunteers and activists should be aware and keep on top of the issue.

Case Study – Claire Wright

Claire Wright is an Independent County Councillor for Otter Valley, Devon, and has stood in the last two general elections, hoping to be the UK's first female Independent MP. She was also elected to East Devon District Council in May 2011, standing down in 2015.

Claire traces her first campaign back to her childhood, when aged nine she wrote to the Brazilian Embassy demanding that they stopped killing dolphins for their eyeballs. This thread carried on through a career in public relations and the NHS, until she found her calling as an Independent county councillor. In this capacity, she finds she can speak freely, unfettered by party politics, putting her constituents' needs first and foremost, without pressure to think or vote along party lines.

In the past, she has campaigned against supermarket developments, protected the right to stay overnight at a local maternity unit, ensured a play park was built despite a funding shortfall, encouraged BT Openreach to improve its broadband service in the area, encouraged local council transparency and openness, and fought over-development. She is also campaigning against a proposed quarry that would devastate ancient woodland and increase HGV traffic, and supports the lowering of the UK voting age to 16.

In her capacity as Devon County Councillor, Claire keeps a keen eye on proposed changes to community hospitals and is campaigning for a cycleway working with cycling charity, Sustrans. She is also the Woodland Trust's Tree Champion for Devon, successfully persuading Devon County Council to carry out more tree planting, and leads a pilot scheme to encourage more wildflowers in the county.

A dedicated team of volunteers supported Claire during her General Election bids, with a parliamentary team of about twelve, and a wider team of hundreds of leafleters. The support of this team was 'vital' says Claire, adding that after both her bids for Parliament, she felt quite bereft 'of their company and have had to readjust to not working day to day with such a brilliant group of people who end up as my friends'. Claire explains that running for Parliament as an Independent is a 'massive task', and that she gained 'expertise, energy, passion, enthusiasm and a shared purpose' from her supporters, and was able to share out the workload.

When asked how she motivates others to campaign alongside her, Claire believes that many of her supporters found working with an Independent exciting because she was offering 'something different to the norm'; she also thinks being down-to-earth, honest, straightforward and appreciative helps. For her, the key to developing campaigning relationships is to 'stay grounded and careful about team happiness'. She thinks it's easy for little tensions to develop because the format for working as an Independent is 'new and flexible', so it's important to resolve any difficulties before they develop. She also says being appreciative is very important, because the team needs to feel valued.

Claire is the first to admit she is very touched when people tell her she has inspired them, or given them hope or motivation to get out and vote or help a candidate for the first time. She adds that it 'is especially rewarding when young people say I have inspired them'.

Takeaways

- Are you passionate enough about something to want to make a difference?
- Could you help with existing projects and campaigns to achieve your goals?
- What are your strengths – and could they help a team project?
- What skills do you lack that others might bring to a campaign?
- Are you approachable? If you want to create a team, or work with one, you'll need to make sure you are.
- Could you manage a diverse team – and make the most of individual skillsets?

4

Getting Organised

Take yourself seriously

A sporty person I know is given to saying 'Fail to plan, and plan to fail' as she preps for an important race or event – and it's a philosophy I like to apply in other aspects of my life. Similarly, you should approach your activism, advocacy or campaigning using the same level of organisation as you would if you had a work or personal plan you wanted to put into action.

When planning your campaign with your team, it's worth putting some thought into the following topics:

- What are our goals?
- What are the 'stepping stones' we can use to achieve those goals?
- What are our strengths and weaknesses?
- How can we maximise our potential?
- Who are we trying to reach?
- Which influencers must we target?

Structure your campaign

Answering the questions above will allow you to structure your campaign, make the most of the skillset of your team by assigning appropriate tasks, avoid any duplication of work, involve everyone who has come forward, and boost morale and, in turn, the involvement of those working with and alongside you. This professionalism will pay dividends when you need to discuss your campaign with others – be that for media coverage, to encourage support or to put your case across to lawmakers and other influencers.

And while it might seem rather formal to call regular campaign meetings, complete with a written agenda and minutes to circulate, it's an incredibly successful way to evaluate what you are doing well and what you have learned along the way. Should you ever be criticised or investigated (the latter is unlikely, of course, but it pays to be prepared), a record of effectively structured meetings will also demonstrate your professionalism.

Meetings can cover day-to-day details, keep everyone updated with progress and dish out new tasks with clear ownership and deadlines. They are also a chance to meet the full team in a more social setting, share ideas and inspiration. They offer an opportunity to congratulate each other on individual and group wins, or deal with any challenges the team are facing both alone and together.

When calling meetings, however, bear in mind that, for volunteers, time and money to socialise might be restricted, so you should offer a range of places and times to meet from evenings in the pub to coffee and cake at someone's home or another free venue during the day. Your fellow campaigners should never feel obliged to come, and some may not be able to because of other commitments, but remember to invite everyone, be flexible and ensure all interested parties are kept in the loop by circulating a quick summary and minutes by email after the event.

Why committees work

When there's a group of people who all want to achieve the same thing – it's common to form a committee – assigning each person a role suited to their abilities that they can take ownership for. Typical roles include:

- Chair – the person who oversees a committee meeting; they should be adept at dealing with all the personalities involved
- Secretary – to take minutes and manage any paperwork and communication

- Treasurer – typically in charge of financial management, and also a 'watchdog' to ensure good practice

Some committees might also benefit from:

- Social secretary – to organise social events
- Communications – a person in charge of marketing and media communication
- Fundraising – it is also useful to have someone oversee fundraising

Within informal committees, roles can also be fluid, with the task of minute-taking, for example, floating between members to share the load.

Committees from hell

From an organisational point of view, nothing beats a committee for effectively divvying up work, providing accountability and setting responsibilities and deadlines, but the phrase often has negative connotations. We've all sat in long, dull meetings, whether at work or elsewhere, where nothing is achieved or agreed upon, or where one person or group of people with the same opinion and objectives dominate the entire proceedings. That is not the type of committee you're aiming for!

The Chair should take particular care that any committee meetings are run with focus and fairness, encouraging everyone to participate, speak AND listen. In order for this to happen, it's important that before a meeting an agenda is established, giving everyone a chance to add items for discussion. The agenda should then be adhered to during the meeting, and the Chair should intervene if discussions go too far off course.

While all the ideas listed below might not apply to you and your campaign, a typical meeting agenda should include items such as this:

- Header, including details of meeting date, start and end time, venue, participants
- Chair's welcome
- Approval of minutes of last meeting; checking them through to ensure that everyone is happy with what was recorded
- Budget statement; cataloguing what money has come in, what has been spent and outlining expected upcoming costs
- Matters arising; issues/subjects left over from the previous meeting
- Any Other Business (AOB); a time to open up the meeting to anyone who wants to have input
- Date/location for next meeting

Try to send out your agenda forty-eight hours ahead of the meeting to allow everyone to have their input and to prepare adequately. In addition to the agenda, it's wise to include a copy of the last meeting's minutes and any other supporting documents that might be discussed.

On the record

Part and parcel of running a campaign is the paperwork you'll amass! During your work, you might uncover interesting articles in the press or collect your own media coverage clippings. You might find stats from an agency such as the local Trading Standards or health services, reports on the likely impact of issues as wide-ranging as a housing development or a cut in funding. You might build witness accounts and other evidence, and hone in on information you need to keep safe, refer to or pass on as required. You will need this information to be both accessible and organised for practical reasons. If there is a legal issue, you may need to show that your views are supported and that due diligence has been taken. Nothing beats the feeling of having the documents or data that reinforce your argument at your fingertips.

Maintaining an efficient system for all the records you collect is, therefore, a must. The minutes of any committee meetings you have will naturally form part of this, recording what has been agreed, what has happened and what your plans are going forward. Ringbinders and index cards provide a simple solution, but it's also worth ensuring that all paper records are also held digitally, and perhaps in several locations in case of accidental damage or loss. You'll never regret a back-up!

Delegate the important task of keeping, maintaining, updating and protecting data and information to one or two individuals who will relish the task of finding order in the chaos.

Case Study – Usman Mohammed, Organise

Executive Director Nat Whalley started Organise in 2017 because she 'didn't see anywhere for people who spot problems at work to proactively fix them'. It's now a community of 50,000 people who have free access to a set of decentralised digital tools to help with workplace concerns and, in the past, has helped with employment issues at ITV, McDonald's and Tesco.

The tools allow everyone from Amazon warehouse workers to university academics to team up confidently and take collective action at their work on a confidential basis. It exists to help people start, run and win campaigns that challenge and change the workplace. And the power of Organise lies in its ability to help co-workers team up.

Usman Mohammed is Lead Campaigner at Organise. He explains that the group was set up as collective action seemed to have slipped out of the public consciousness, with union membership on the decline and less awareness generally about how to change things in the working environment. To enable engagement, the group has engineered a free app called TakeNote that allows you to document sexual harassment and bullying in the workplace. This secure bank of evidence can then be downloaded and sent to a lawyer, union rep or the Human Resources department of your employer. In March 2019, Organise was able to reveal that Ted Baker staff had used its campaigning tools to call out CEO Ray Kelvin for alleged harassment. Kelvin resigned[2] amid allegations of 'forced hugging'[3] and other inappropriate behaviour.

Usman has plenty of advice for campaigners, and says the 'first and most important step' to planning a campaign should always be listening to 'the very personal, human, emotional, uncomplicated problems that the things we're trying to stop often throw up.' Framing campaigns in the voices of those affected, he argues, will decide whether your campaign finds its feet or not. Examples might be a call to implement a fairer holiday booking system at work or paid leave for someone affected by domestic violence.

The most important part of the campaign, he believes, is the message, which he describes as 'the narrative drive of why something needs to change', adding that sometimes that's expressed most powerfully by the average person. After listening to the problem, he recommends 'using as much of the language you hear as possible'.

[2] https://www.theguardian.com/business/2019/mar/04/ted-baker-boss-ray-kelvin-quits
[3] https://www.theguardian.com/business/2018/dec/02/ted-baker-staff-complain-forced-hugs-company-founder-ray-kelvin

Then think in terms of a 'powermap' – decide who all the stakeholders in the campaign are and put these on a grid that plots how much they agree with you on one axis, against how powerful they are on another axis. He adds, 'There's a huge difference between being right and being effective – bear that in mind when thinking about tactics.'

He also recommends using other experienced campaigners 'as signposts' to direct your way and, if you're planning a meeting, to ensure they have a distinct timed purpose and a clear objective.

Takeaways

- It's key to use professional organisational skills within your campaign
- Your aim is to document evidence that will support your cause
- Listen to those directly affected by the issue and use their observations to frame your campaign
- Make your campaign message 'human' – so that people can engage emotionally
- Decide who are the stakeholders in your campaign
- Learn from other experienced campaigners
- Being right and being effective are two different things

5

Gathering Information

What can research do for you?
When you are trying to change or improve a system, you often have to work from within that system, or at least according to its established rules, to make a difference. It's therefore imperative that before you go in all guns blazing, you take some time to understand the system, the important players within it and the hierarchy there. Learn all you can about how things work, what motivates the people involved, how changes are normally made and what processes exist for accountability and complaints. Taking the time to learn about the processes and factors involved will allow you to set clear goals and create a network of useful contacts.

Questions to ask include:

- Who is in charge?
- How many people combine to make a decision?
- Are there regulations or guidelines that must be followed?
- Are there laws that must be obeyed?
- Is the system transparent?
- Have there been complaints?
- Who handles complaints?
- How have concerns been addressed?
- Who can make change happen?

Specific examples of where this approach is necessary include local and national government; in the health, immigration, benefits and education systems; within the workplace; and within the police force, too.

Large campaigns that aim to change behaviour and attitudes in society as a whole also benefit from a considered approach. While it's just as likely that local and national policies are directing the public to think in a certain way, campaigns that target social issues can be harder to tackle because there might not be one clear change to campaign for, rather an entire system of beliefs or habits. However, thorough research into why the public or consumers act or purchase in a certain way will still be an essential precursor to setting your campaign goals.

How to convince people you're right

If you're planning on making a change, it's highly likely you'll need to win people over and talk them round to your way of thinking. You might want to encourage the public or a certain section of the public to change its behaviour; you might need to lobby for an event or action to be cancelled; you might hope to convince an official to change the law. And to be persuasive, you're going to need some evidence to base your arguments upon. Yet again, doing your research can pay dividends.

You will need:

- Facts – objective things that are known or have been proven to be true
- Statistics – mathematical equations that can be used to show trends, typically used in finding averages, rates and medians
- Data – facts and statistics collected together for reference or analysis
- Opinions – while first-person experiences and reactions can make an argument 'real', opinions are not always believed

Typically, facts and figures are viewed as more believable than opinions – and can be used as powerful pieces of evidence to strengthen your argument. Data captures the attention and imagination of the public and can emphasise your point. If presented in an easily digestible form, it allows your audience to understand a complex issue quickly. Simple facts and stats are also tremendously popular with the media as it means that a story can be presented as a simple snapshot, often turned into a visual aid that breaks up text or speech. This may be the ideal task for the maths genius of your team.

But remember
As useful as it is, data must be relevant and relatable for an audience to understand and retain it. Instead of trotting out a collection of unintelligible numbers, you should look to express figures in a way that allows people to compare it to something they do understand. For example, instead of talking about the height of a proposed building that you oppose, liken it to something they can visualise more easily such as the equivalent number of double-decker buses; as an alternative to quoting the number of people using a particular service, such as a local food bank, why not express it as the same size population of a well-known city. And if you're preparing a presentation or press pack, you can easily use graphics to illustrate examples such as this.

A tongue-in-cheek media convertor is available from The Register[4], and conveniently allows you to express commonly-used metric and imperial standards in terms of everything from the size of a football pitch to the weight of a Great White Shark.

Bear in mind, however, statistics can be misleading – see the phenomenally successful 2001 book *Damned Lies and Statistics* by Joel Best – so never accept them blindly. Always ask if your evidence comes from a reliable source – think 'Who asked?' and 'Who paid?' This especially applies to research found on the Internet.

[4] https://www.theregister.co.uk/Design/page/reg-standards-converter.html

Sourcing information

A great way to monitor the media for up-to-date coverage of an issue is by setting up Google Alerts. This is a content detection and notification service, offered by the search engine company Google. The service sends emails to the user when it finds new results that match the user's specified search term.

Results include everything from web pages and media articles to blogs and scientific research. Alerts can be set to track companies, organisations, people, products and topics – even yourself!

The process is simple:

- Go to google.com/alerts in your browser
- Enter a search term for the topic you want to track
- Choose 'Show Options' to narrow the alert to a specific source, language, and/or region
- Select 'Create Alert'

You'll receive emails with hotlinks to relevant online news and articles direct to your inbox.

Hashtags

Social media is a great place to follow topics and garner information. Why not follow a hashtag (#) on Twitter by setting up a saved search? Search for your chosen hashtag, then look for the three vertical dots on the right of the results screen (officially called the 'overflow icon') and select 'Save this search'. The next time you tap the search box, a pop-up menu will display your saved searches. It's good for twenty-five searches per account.

You can also follow a hashtag on Instagram by tapping on any one that you see on the platform. Once you've done this, relevant posts appear in your feed automatically. Within Facebook, you can search for a hashtag using the search bar at the top of any page.

Non-profit organisations

Non-profit organisations (sometimes also called not-for-profit organisations) is a broad term for all independent organisations whose purpose is something other than to make private profit for directors, members or shareholders. They can take many forms. The one thing they all have in common, however, is their advocacy role. The Royal College of Nursing is a not-for-profit organisation, as well as a nursing union and professional body. Food and farming charity and organic certification body, The Soil Association, is also a not-for-profit, along with the Rainbow Trust children's charity, which provides emotional and practical support to families who have a child with a life-threatening or terminal illness; the conservation charity and zoo Marwell Wildlife is another such organisation. Many housing associations are also non-profits.

Not all non-profits are registered charities, but all organisations with charity status are by nature non-profits. One of the UK's top charities (measured in terms of donations and reported in the *Guardian* newspaper) is 'Gavi', the Vaccine Alliance, which draws together major international bodies to fund immunisation programmes; others on the list include major health charities such as Cancer Research UK and Macmillan, global development groups Save the Children, Oxfam and the British Red Cross, and animal charities such as the RSPCA and the RSPB.

Advice and help

What many non-profits have in common is that they will fund and/or organise research projects, collating evidence that will help them and others working for the same cause to reach their objectives. The results of these projects are often shared with the media and with others who can benefit from them.

As such, these organisations are a treasure trove of facts and figures, freely available to use to support your cause. Many of the non-profits will have websites that you can search to obtain information. Some will also offer helplines or other ways to get in touch if you cannot find what you are looking for.

Freedom of information (FOI)

One of the best tools in the box for campaigners is the current FOI Act, which gives everyone regardless of age, nationality or location the right to access recorded information held by public-sector organisations. This includes organisations such as:

- Government departments and other public bodies and committees
- Local councils
- Schools, colleges and universities
- Health trusts, hospitals and doctors' surgeries
- Publicly owned companies
- Publicly funded museums
- The police

Government departments and other bodies often publish responses to previous freedom of information requests online, too, which you can check at www.gov.uk.

Since its inception, the FOI Act has been used to release a great deal of information that was in the public interest but had previously been unavailable. In 2009, the FOI act was used to reveal the expenses claimed by MPs – which included the infamous claim of £1,645 by Sir Peter Viggers for a floating duck house in the garden pond at his constituency home. Other high-profile requests have revealed how much public money was spent on police to cover football matches, which car brands fail most often at MOTs, if a police knife amnesty in London actually reduced knife crime and what the average wait was for an emergency ambulance.

How to make an FOI request

To make an FOI request, you'll need to contact the organisation you want to approach in writing. This can be done via letter, email or an online form, ideally found on the organisation's website. You'll need to include the following information:

- Your name (not needed if requesting environmental information)
- A postal or email address for the reply
- A detailed description of the information you want – ensure your request clearly specifies what information you require
- A clear instruction if you need the reply in a particular format – for example, large print or audio

You can find out if the information is already available by checking the published responses to previous FOI requests on www.gov.uk and government publications. You can also simply ring the organisation and ask if the details are available. In most cases your request should be free – although you may be asked to pay a fee to cover postage.

Getting an answer

In theory, an answer to an FOI request under the Freedom of Information Act should reach you in twenty working days, unless the organisation has informed you it will take longer. When you send your request, make a note of the date or keep a copy of it. In some cases, a delayed reply will be for a credible reason, such as the need for different people to be contacted to obtain the information or because a test for public interest exemption has been considered and applied.

If, however, you have heard nothing after twenty working days of receipt, you should email the organisation and ask why you haven't had a reply within the statutory time limit. If your email also receives no response, follow it up with a phone call, ideally to the department that would deal with the request. DON'T GIVE UP! Persistence is often the key.

If you are still not being given the information or any advice as to why there is a delay, you can complain directly to the Information Commissioner's Office (ICO), which is the independent authority charged with promoting openness by public bodies. Try the helpline – 0303 123 1113 – or use the Live Chat facility on its website (www.ico.org.uk).

Case Study – Hugo Sugg

Hugo Sugg is a campaigner for better support for the homeless. He is also the founder of Hugo's Earthquake, which aims to challenge the public perception of homelessness and rough sleeping and creates campaigns that help promote an understanding of why and how people become homeless. The campaign also lobbies for better services for homeless people and legislation protecting them.

It was created in 2015 and its biggest project to date is its 'Justice for Cardon' campaign. The campaign began after the death of Cardon Banfield, a 74-year-old homeless man who was part of the Windrush Generation and came to the UK in 1961 from St Vincent and the Grenadines. On 5 July 2016, Cardon's body was found on the banks of the River Severn, but as it was 'partially mummified' it took months to identify him. Hugo's Earthquake has been working to ensure that people and organisations are held accountable for the systemic chain of events that led both to the tragedy and the difficulty in obtaining a Safeguarding Adults Review.

Hugo Sugg says collating and providing information

is an important part of campaigning because it informs your message and helps tell people what you are trying to do and how you are trying to do it. Finding relevant information 'is vital to gaining credibility', he explains. 'Research and information may help people support your campaign and encourage them to share information from your cause on their social media – meaning others can find out about the campaign and follow/support it if they wish.'

Hugo recommends sourcing facts and figures to use in your campaign from the Government, healthcare system or charities related to your cause. He advises being clear about what you are looking for, as this will help you search through information and pick out things that are relevant to your campaign/cause and discard that which is not. For best practice, Hugo recommends checking facts and figures from several rather than one single source.

Hugo says the use of FOI requests has been critical in the #JusticeForCardon campaign, helping to reveal the decisions made prior to Cardon's death. Hugo explains that FOI requests can help uncover information from a public body that isn't in the public domain, and can 'be what results in a successful/achieved campaign'. He also says that the information you don't get – 'which happens a lot also' – can be vital in growing and building on your campaign, as you can submit another FOI, worded differently, to get a different set of information or statistics/facts.

His advice for penning a successful FOI request includes 'being very specific in your wording in relation to what information you want', because the more specific you make it, the sooner you will be able to get an answer to your request without going through 'weeks and weeks of back-and-forth emails'. If you know the department responsible for the information, Hugo would also recommend including that on your request, so the FOI team can direct the enquiry to the right people.

And if you are doing a follow-up FOI to one you got back, Hugo also recommends referencing the previous request and adding in what further information you'd like. 'Try and make this as succinct as possible,' he warns, 'because a public body could reasonably refuse an FOI request on the grounds of it being repetitive or vexatious if you put in lots at the same time for the same information.'

Hugo also says that simply Googling the particular issue he's campaigning on and clicking on 'News' helps him keep up to date on an issue. He also follows council committee meetings and sends emails, submits FOI's and talks to members of staff who work in the homeless sector in Worcestershire to find out information for the #JusticeForCardon campaign.

The Hugo's Earthquake Campaign also has volunteer press officers and researchers who work together to find out the latest on the issue of homelessness and then share this information on social media.

Takeaways

- Collating and providing relevant information brings credibility to your campaign
- People feel more able to support and share your campaign when it is backed by well-researched information
- To help you focus your search, be clear which facts and figures you need at the start
- Use more than one source to ensure authority
- Take time to plan FOI requests, wording them carefully to save time and maximise results

Part II

Getting People
to Take Notice

6

Spreading The Message

What is your message?

When you first find something you want to change, it can be hard to understand and decide which key element or elements are the crux of the problem. It's also difficult to decide which is the most important part of your campaign. It's like the proverbial chicken and egg question. However, if you've spent some time following the advice in Chapters 2 and 4, you should have a clearer idea of what you want to change, who or what can make that change happen and the audience you plan to target with your message.

The next step is to get to work spreading that message to interested and affected parties and to those who can really make a change. To do this you will need to develop and focus on a core message or messages – one or several simple sentences that sum up what the problem is and what the campaign aims to do or change. The idea is to open up conversations about the issue you're sharing and build relationships with more and more supporters. Core messages encapsulate the big idea at the heart of your campaign, they help everyone who listens to understand and engage with your work. Your message must be articulate and consistent.

Ask yourself, 'What do I want people to remember about my campaign?'

The basis of all your communications

Effectively, core messages are the first chance to get people on side. They are a bit like an 'elevator pitch' in business – succinct and persuasive. And since, let's face it, most people have short attention spans, without an effective core message your audience is likely to misunderstand and/or lose interest. Your core message will form the basis of all your communications when you talk or write about your campaign or deal with the media and other organisations, reinforcing your aims and goals.

Here's a quick three-step process to help you decide what your message or messages should be:

- Identify the need or challenge you are facing
- Outline your solution or approach
- Describe the positive results

The idea behind your message is that it motivates others. You need to look at it from their point of view and find a way that makes them care enough to support the campaign. Remember, the most important thing is not how witty or clever it is, but what the recipient gets out of it.

Try and keep your message simple as providing too much information can be counter-productive, confusing and boring. Also, avoid inconsistency at all costs, particularly if several people in your campaign team are involved in spreading your message. To avoid this, you could identify one of your team as the official spokesperson and direct all enquiries to this person.

Message methods

There are several ways to sum up and transmit your message, and perhaps one the most versatile is the use of a slogan. Once you've decided on a snappy yet informative slogan, you can use it on everything from protest banners and car stickers to written and spoken media interviews. Some of the best-known and successful campaigns have used slogans. Here are some examples that have stuck in my mind for years:

- 'Make love, not war' (USA anti-Vietnam protests, 1960s)

- 'Think globally, act locally' (Friends of the Earth, 1969)
- 'Clunk-click every trip' (British public service announcement, 1970)
- 'A dog is for life, not just for Christmas' (Dog's Trust, 1978)
- 'AIDS – don't die of ignorance' (Department of Health and Social Security, 1986)
- 'We'd rather go naked than wear fur' (Peta, 1994)
- 'Some people are gay – Get over it' (Stonewall, 2007)
- 'Girls just want to have FUNdamental human rights' (Women's March, 2017)

Another great example of a successful slogan that captured the attention of the media and the public was used in December 1982 by the Greenham Common protestors. Around 30,000 members of the Women's Peace Camp stood linking hands around the nine-mile perimeter of the site that held US cruise missiles in the 'Embrace the Base' demonstration – and photographers clamoured to get shots.

Easy-to-remember activism quotes also became part of fashion culture when in 1984 Katharine Hamnett met Margaret Thatcher. The outspoken designer famously unzipped her jacket to reveal a politically charged t-shirt saying: '58 per cent don't want Pershing', in an anti-nuclear statement. The designs became iconic and were incredibly popular in the 1980s, with hoards of copycat designs still on the market today. Even our 'Stop Pet Shop Pups' protests had an accompanying t-shirt declaring 'Free the Puppies'. If you check the news reports covering the #LucysLaw marches, meetings, rallies and PupAid events we participated in, you'll see us effectively reinforcing that message time and time again.

Hello hashtags
Perhaps a more modern form of the slogan is the hashtag – basically a word or phrase with the hash symbol (#) placed before it. Hashtags

were designed for use on social media websites and applications, especially Twitter, to identify messages on a specific topic, appearing online from about 2007. They are designed to be searchable, so that when you search a hashtag on a social media platform all the posts with that hashtag appear. In fact, they are so popular and effective that spammers will deliberately add popular hashtags to their posts even when it's not relevant. Hashtags are now so ubiquitous that they virtually stand alone as a campaign marker.

Since hashtags can drive a lot of online traffic to your posts and raise awareness, it's worth choosing them carefully. Ideally, your hashtag would need to be original (so you're not getting confused or merged with another organisation), precise and easy-to-understand. The aim is for your hashtag to 'go viral' – which means that it spreads quickly and is shared frequently – and encourages your audience to adopt it themselves each time they post.

Look to use three or four words that run together, using title case to aid easy reading and avoid the infamous mistake made by the promoters of the #SusanAlbumParty (which can be read very differently without capital letters: #susanalbumparty). You'll also want to avoid ending up with a 'Bashtag', which has happened to many a commercial enterprise looking for a bit of self-promotion. For example, when McDonald's came up with the #McDStories hashtag it was expecting customers to add engaging happy memories; instead, customers and haters posted about bad experiences with the brand and its ethics. It's worth showing your hashtag to a few people unconnected to your campaign for a second opinion before you go public.

Used correctly, however, hashtags enable activists to give their campaign long-term momentum, increasing awareness and familiarity, encouraging engagement. Remember to use your chosen hashtag frequently. Here are some great examples of hashtags that have boosted a campaign positively:

#BlackLivesMatter

The #BlackLivesMatter hashtag appeared on social media in 2013 after the acquittal of George Zimmerman for the shooting of African-American teen Trayvon Martin a year earlier. Martin was walking back to the house of his father's fiancée when Zimmerman, a member of the community watch, met him. There was a confrontation and Martin was fatally shot in the chest, which Zimmerman claimed was in self-defence. The hashtag resulted in the formation of a civil rights movement designed to fight institutionalised racism across the United States, with more than twenty-six Black Lives Matter chapters across the country campaigning for equal rights for all Americans.

#IceBucketChallenge

ALS Association's campaign in the summer of 2014 had Facebook newsfeeds filled with videos of people tipping icy water over themselves (including me!). In the UK, one in six people took part and because the challenge required people to nominate their friends, the momentum kept going. In turn, the #IceBucketChallenge raised awareness about ALS (also known as motor neurone disease) and it raised money for the ALS Association, the Motor Neurone Disease Association and other charities. Perhaps most interestingly, its inception is not credited to either of the charities that benefited, rather to American students raising money after their own diagnoses.

#StopFundingHate

This grassroots campaign was launched in August 2016, in response to negative headlines about migrants and refugees that activists saw in the media. Fearing negative media coverage would lead to hate crime, the instigators set about persuading advertisers to pull their support from the publications they felt spread hate and division – specifically the *Daily Mail,* the *Sun* and the *Daily Express* newspapers. The campaign encourages consumers to take pictures of advertisers they spot in the papers and tweet them to ask them to pull their sponsorship. The campaign has had major success with Lego and The Body Shop cutting ties. Under new editorship, the *Daily Express* saw a substantial drop in front-page headlines covering refugees, so the paper has been taken off the active target list and placed under review instead.

Speak to your friends

Once you have your core messages, be they slogans or hashtags or both, the next step is to take your fight out into the wild. An easy place to start is with your immediate network – your friends and family, the people you know, the groups you attend, the communities where you are already a stakeholder both online and off. Never be afraid to ask if you can discuss your campaign and views with people and with groups – you've already mapped out what you want to say so you can be confident that you are clear and knowledgeable. No doubt you'll be surprised at how others can help you, with further useful contacts, more information and eagerness to share your views for the greater good. Generally, people are more likely to engage with something they feel involved in, so don't be scared to ask for help. And say thank you, too, because it's a further way to maintain that positive relationship (and because it's the right thing to do anyway).

Build a community

In order to secure wider coverage, you'll need to build a community. A key element to this is that it must allow dialogue between you and your supporters, as well as potential supporters. This is why a blog or a website or a social media presence works so well, because it allows that all-important two-way communication and relationship-building you'll need to achieve your goals.

While each of these approaches is covered more thoroughly in later chapters, there's an easy way to remember what you're aiming for — the three Is:

- Attract their **INTEREST** through some form of entertainment
- Give them **INFORMATION** – be the expert on this topic, the one-stop-shop for all current news, research etc.
- **INSPIRE** them to get involved – show why this is important and relatable to them, and encourage an emotional response by sharing your passion

Events

Fun social events, outreach, educational workshops and fundraisers are ways to interact with more people and spread your reach. Consider everything from a pub quiz or sporting event to an attempt to set an unusual world record. For example, children's brain tumour cancer charity Anna's Hope attracted 878 people to set the world record for the largest gathering of fairies.

Casual events allow you to be seen as real people rather than campaigners. Use these events as a chance to engage in conversation and connect with new supporters, and to build a community around your cause. Choose locations and themes that have a natural affinity for your cause to encourage like-minded people to get involved. Events are also great for publicity, particularly if you can get the local media to list, cover and/or attend.

VIPs

Another great way to draw people into your campaign, is to ask experts, high-profile individuals and celebrities to join you at events you host, and to support you online via social media shares, likes, follows and other endorsements. A familiar face – or one whose opinion and work the public respects – functions well because it hooks people's attention and then helps the public to remember a campaign. When someone we admire endorses a viewpoint, we are more likely to agree with it.

Commercial brands spend millions hiring celebs to promote their products because they bring with them huge numbers of fans. Likewise, a carefully chosen individual – whether famous in the general celebrity sense or an individual who is well known in certain circles – can bring more supporters into the fold. Some recent examples include Joanna Lumley lobbying for the Gurkhas; Emma Thompson and Alistair McGowan buying land to block the third runway at Heathrow; and stand-up comedian Josie Long who supports the UK Uncut movement, a network of protest groups that oppose cuts to public services and UK tax avoidance.

Now you've established your message and a plan to disperse it far and wide, you'll also need to think about PR.

Case Study – Melissa Mead MBE

Melissa lost her son William to sepsis just after his first birthday in December 2014. Since then, she has campaigned to raise awareness of the disease among both the public and medical professionals.

Melissa's successes in her campaign include the significant rise in the number of people who are now aware of sepsis; more than 70 per cent of the population are now able to say they've heard of it compared to just over 30 per cent several years ago. The increase in reported cases of sepsis suggests more accurate diagnoses are taking place, with faster access to appropriate care.

With more than 70 per cent of cases of sepsis arising in the community, as opposed to in hospitals, Melissa knew she had to take the message out to society as a whole, covering all demographics. Her audience is the entire nation, but that can be subdivided into healthcare professionals and the public, then the public into adults and adults who are also parents. Her message has been shared via appearances on television and radio, and with pieces in magazines, newspapers, on the news and social media.

Television adverts and storylines in soaps and radio shows have further helped. There has also been indirect messaging in places of work, schools, dentists' and GPs' surgeries, pharmacies, out-of-hours units and acute centres, too.

Melissa works with the UK Sepsis Trust charity as an ambassador and spokesperson. The charity helps the media ensure that the terminology and language used in storylines is correct and communicated efficiently. Getting the message across to TV audiences accesses seven million viewers in one impressive and effective hit.

While Melissa never set out to be a campaigner, William's story exploded in the national press in January 2016, after the report into his death was published. She found herself 'catapulted on to a large platform' and says that she 'grabbed every opportunity with both hands'. The campaign snowballed and Melissa makes sure to build relationships in all different arenas, engaging with everyone, because 'ultimately, awareness is about starting a conversation'.

Talking, sharing, writing and 'grabbing every

opportunity presented to me and never turning anything down' is how Melissa keeps her campaign going. She talks extensively to people in the healthcare industry in order to change attitudes and behaviours and ensure that cases of sepsis aren't missed. She also keeps the message clear, concise and engaging, using hashtags and slogans to create trends and measure impact, such as using #KissGoodbyeToSepsis around Valentine's Day.

She also uses facts and figures to communicate effectively. The statistics – someone, somewhere in the world will die of sepsis every 3.5 seconds – are hard-hitting and sell themselves.

While Melissa regards her MBE as recognition of the impact her campaign has had – and continues to have – nationwide, her work is her 'way of being William's mum', with her passion and dedication coming from both love and grief. For Melissa, 'William is the message'. She explains that, just like any other parent, she wants to talk about her children, and that sharing William's story enables her to do just that, adding, 'I am not defined by the little boy who died but the little boy who lived.'

For Melissa, however, the real success is the lives her work has saved. She says the most rewarding thing about her campaigning has been 'absolutely and most definitely, getting a message from someone to say, "Because of you, my son, my wife etc. are alive." I get quite a few messages of that nature and they never fail to floor me and give me goosebumps. That is a real, tangible effect of the work I seek to do.'

Takeaways

- Consider which demographic you need to take your message to – can it be subdivided by age, gender, profession or lifestyle?
- Your aim is to spread your message as wide as you can among your targeted audience
- Ask if the media could help raise awareness of your campaign
- Would coverage on TV, radio, the press or social media be appropriate?
- Is there a larger organisation you could work with? Perhaps a charity or NGO?
- Hashtags can help communicate your message effectively
- Facts and figures are also a useful sell
- Be ready to grab every opportunity you can

7

PR

What exactly is PR?

Public Relations – more often just referred to as PR – is the practice of managing the spread of information between an individual or organisation and the public. It's also the voluntary-worker cousin of advertising and, as the old saying goes: 'Advertising is what you pay for, PR is what you pray for'. It's a strategic skill employed to ensure positive, unpaid (or 'earned', if you like) coverage, resulting in everything from space in traditional and social media to appearances at events and conferences. And that's not to say you don't have to pay for the PR services you use, just that it works differently from the straightforward transactional nature of advertising. PR targets effective opportunities for reaching the general public.

PR affects all individuals, organisations and businesses that are in touch with the public, whatever the size. Customers, suppliers, employees, investors, journalists and regulators all form an opinion of the organisations they come into contact with, an opinion they will readily share and use to make decisions about working with, funding or buying from that organisation. That's why PR is also connected in part to the concept of reputation, and why the UK's Chartered Institute of Public Relations defines the art as 'the result of what you do, what you say and what others say about you'.

This means that strong and successful PR should look after your reputation – sympathetically teaching stakeholders about your values, building positive relationships and hoping to gain support, with the ultimate aim of influencing both opinion and behaviour. For a retail business, this is the process of letting the consumer know your product is available, that it is a quality item from a trustworthy source, and then motivating the consumer to go out and buy that product. And in campaigning, as in business, your reputation can be your biggest asset, setting you apart from others and giving you a competitive edge.

What can PR do for me?

When you invest time, and perhaps even money, into PR you should expect to see the following in return:

- An identity highlighting the key elements of your campaign
- Recognition and awareness among the general public
- Growing trust – developing credibility over time
- Opportunities for building support via two-way engagement

Is PR relevant to activism?

Typically, PR is thought of as something a business spends its cash on to help drive sales; however, organisations ranging from government bodies, public services, charities and voluntary groups can also benefit from raising their profile, gaining exposure and cultivating a positive relationship with those it hopes – and needs – to influence. Activists must also learn to harness the power of good PR to gain exposure, spread their messages and ultimately bring about the change they are campaigning for.

And let's not forget that PR can also help organisations defend their reputation during a crisis that threatens their credibility. It's not uncommon for activists to receive 'bad press' from people who would be threatened by a successful campaign and people who don't understand why anyone would challenge the status quo. Thankfully, PR can also be used to mitigate this sort of damage.

What PR isn't

In the digital age, PR can include content, relationships and engagement, so its definitions are a little blurry, but it is important to understand what PR is not. PR is not marketing, advertising, selling or promotion, disciplines that are principally involved in moving a product or an idea through a pipeline, selling it via paid adverts, negotiations with potential customers and tools such as 'Buy One Get One Free' (BOGOFs) to encourage take-up. PR is also not guaranteed, a quick fix or a way to get free advertising. And while we're at it, we should also dispel the myth that PR is easy and that anyone can do it!

Instead, PR is about building long-term relationships with the end result being your campaign, spokesperson, core values or expertise you espouse featuring in the media. It works best when coverage extends beyond your reach, adding to your credibility and informing your audience without a hard sell. And because of that, PR should be a two-way process. To be effective at PR, an organisation must listen to the opinions of those with whom it deals, and not solely deliver information to the general public.

Storytelling

How does one portray a reputation, idea, product or position? By using one of the most powerful skills a PR can possess – the art of telling stories. Facts on their own can be dull, but stories can make you laugh, cry, relate and care – evoking feelings strong enough to motivate an individual to go out and do something. Successful PR, therefore, is about looking for the story that will engage the audience *and* bring your campaign message to life. Storytelling of any nature stimulates the brain of the listener – it's the job of PR to find the characters, conflict, tension and resolution that will engage the audience's senses. Many big brands achieve this through the story of their founder – think how important the personality of Richard Branson is to the Virgin brand. The story will attract a journalist but, in order for PR to really work, the story must have an authentic and clear message.

Campaigns are ideal for storytelling as the central issue

usually has human or animal interest, and is often the very reason you started the movement.

Avoid the common mistakes

Unfortunately, not everyone will be as interested in your cause as you are. Your PR strategy should take this into consideration. To ensure you make the most of any PR opportunity, don't miss out on getting coverage by disregarding the longer lead times of traditional media. For example, monthly magazines are often working on issues four months ahead. When you get in touch, use simple language and check for mistakes to ensure an easy-to-read and concise release. Jargon and buzzwords that make an issue hard to understand will count against you, as will latching on to any trend or news story that does not bear any relevance to your own. You've got a limited time to grab an editor's attention so use it wisely! Make sure you are well prepared before making phone calls or attending meetings, and don't be afraid to follow up and always be ready to close the deal.

Your PR toolkit

So what exactly will you need for PR purposes? Here's a list to get you started:

- Photos – provide high-resolution images (at least 1MB) and low-resolution options in different orientations. Depending on your campaign, this might be of people who feature in your story, a setting, a logo or an item. Video content is also a good sell.
- A press release – with an attention-grabbing title, all the key info and full contact details.
- A bio of you/your organisation – similar to an 'About us' page online – with all the key facts and figures.
- A hit list of media outlets to target – but don't turn down any

offers from those not on your list.

- Time – difficult if you're running a campaign in a voluntary capacity but then nothing worth having comes easy.

You'll find more information about approaching the press in chapter 12.

Case Study – Natalie Trice

Natalie's son was diagnosed with hip dysplasia (DDH) nearly ten years ago and she has spent the past decade raising awareness of this common but poorly supported condition, alongside caring for him. She founded DDH UK, a charitable trust that helps thousands of people around the world with DDH and those caring for them.

Natalie is also the author of *Cast Life*, a guide to DDH, the book she wished had existed when she first learnt of her son's condition. She also sits on various medical boards, including those at the International Hip Dysplasia Institute, Great Ormond Street Hospital and Orthopaedic Research UK.

Natalie has extensive PR experience in the business-to-business, broadcast, charity, consumer, corporate and lifestyle sectors, having forged a successful PR career in London. She worked her creative magic for many global companies including Adobe, Animal Planet, Cartoon Network, Discovery Channel, Epson and Hewlett-Packard. In 2007, Natalie struck out on her own, consulting for a range of clients around the UK. She was able to bring her considerable professional experience to her DDH campaigns.

'When used well, PR is an extremely powerful and effective means of communication,' Natalie explains, adding that it can help raise awareness of a cause and fundraise, build profiles, help you to position yourself as an expert in the field, increase sales, and help a charity or cause to build support.

Using her background, Natalie was able to promote her book and the DDH UK charity. However, those who don't have professional experience should not discount doing their own PR, she says, as long as they do their research and understand what they want to achieve. She recommends you decide 'what you are saying, who you are talking to and what you want the outcomes to be. That could be a piece in a local newspaper, a chat on the radio or an interview with an influential blogger.'

However, hiring a PR agency or independent consultant can certainly make your PR efforts more effective, she says, with their expertise and contacts often getting your press release straight to the major players. Professional PRs know who writes about what, when media deadlines are, what images will work, how surveys and case studies can help and so much more. 'If you want a really good job done, get an expert to do it,' she says, but remember that 'PR takes time and skill so don't expect people to do it for nothing, unless they take on pro-bono work and your cause is something that is close their heart'.

To decide if you will see a return for professional PR costs, Natalie suggests setting your goals at the start of your campaign, so that you can measure how successful PR has been. This might mean deciding on a fundraising goal, looking for a petition to reach a certain number of signatures or aiming for a set number of sign-ups to your project.

However, if paying for PR is not an option, Natalie

still has lots of advice. She runs a free Facebook group called 'PR School', which is an informal and supportive network of people who will listen and offer suggestions. She also recommends the charity Media Trust, which can help and advise you, and suggests searching Eventbrite to find suitable activities. And if all else fails, 'hit Google and see what you can find,' she says.

Takeaways

- PR can be powerful and effective, raising awareness of, and building a profile for, your cause
- Consider using PR to position yourself as an expert on the issues at the core of your activism
- Decide what you are saying, who you are talking to and what outcomes you want to achieve
- Don't discount doing your own PR if you have no budget for professional help
- Look for free resources online
- Your PR 'toolkit' should include: images, a press release, 'About us' information and a hit list of media targets

Direct Action

Those who are prepared to take a stand and fight for change shape history. The names of activists such as Gandhi, Martin Luther King, Rosa Parks, Nelson Mandela, Emmeline Pankhurst and Malala Yousafzai are familiar to us all, even if we might be shaky on the precise details of their protests. We teach our children to admire these people and the principles they stood for, and discuss how they worked to make a difference.

Challenge for change

Invariably, success for these pioneering activists relied on their use of various forms of civil resistance using people power and direct action, bringing wider public awareness to their cause and successfully challenging the status quo. This activism, agitation or direct action (and sometimes civil disobedience) took many forms, but can be loosely defined as acts of resistance that undermined the adversary and challenged the system, power or policy. Their activities were often regular, repeated and systematic; sometimes they were symbolic. But their ultimate aim? Change.

What exactly are the different types of direct action and how do they compare to each other?

Marches, rallies and demos

Mass marches are probably the best-known tool in the activist kit. Nothing beats a large turnout of public support, with protestors walking in formation, waving eye-catching banners (who can forget the 'Melania, blink twice if you need help' signs on the women's marches across the globe?) and chanting their demands. Many start or end with speeches and a rally (a mass meeting).

These public meetings or marches might also be called 'demos'.

Of course, large events require organisation and also the correct permissions from local authorities regarding routes to keep everyone safe. Large events have the benefit of often making the papers, not least because they are highly visual and often cause enough disruption to get even the most apathetic individual to look up from their phone. The marches often end at a specific point central to the campaign – such as the regular marches to the Japanese Embassy in London to protest the slaughter of dolphins in Taiji. A significant endpoint plus a speech via a loudhailer are great ways of letting people know what the issue is.

To make an impression with a march or demo, you need a considerable number of people, which is why smaller gatherings are often more useful for protests against a local issue or one with more of a niche audience. Banners and chants are still an essential part of smaller demos and static protests as they are an excellent way to get the message across to anyone passing and even a small number of participants will attract attention.

Vigils

A vigil is an evocative way to call the public's attention to something. The act is associated with the vigil one would keep at the bedside of a sick loved one, so they often carry a sense of sadness. Many activists use vigils to protest inhumane treatment, perhaps of refugees, prisoners or animals (the Save Movement often hold vigils outside slaughterhouses). Vigils are typically peaceful, setting an empathetic tone that makes the protest approachable. They are a good way for a small number of people to make a point; they are media-friendly and banners and speeches can also be employed. Candlelit vigils are an especially good way to attract attention to your cause although, by their nature, they are not a long-lasting protest.

Government buildings, council offices, embassies and the

scenes of accidents or atrocities are common locations for these types of demos. The Kent Anti-Racism Network, for example, organised a vigil in 2019 at the obelisk monument in the town of Ramsgate to welcome migrants to the UK, the area being a hotspot for those trying to cross the English Channel in small boats. The vigil followed a Government decision to launch a 'major incident' after an upsurge in crossings over the Christmas period in 2018, prompting an announcement of an increase in monitoring patrols.

Sit-ins and occupations

A sit-in or sit-down occurs when one or more people occupy an area to protest. They are closely related to occupations, in which a group of people take and hold public and symbolic spaces, buildings and critical infrastructure such as entrances to train stations, shopping centres, university buildings, squares and parks. Sit-ins are typically associated with the civil rights movement as a way to fight racism and segregation but they have also been used effectively by feminist groups, the gun control lobby in the US and by LGBTQ+ rights movements.

Most recently, the grassroots environmental and conservation organisation Extinction Rebellion (sometimes shortened to XR) has come to the fore as advocates of mass civil disobedience. The group argues its protests are the only remaining alternative to address the ecological crisis we face. The group has spearheaded a sit-in at the UK headquarters of Greenpeace, occupied a road in front of the Houses of Parliament and blockaded the Department for Environment, Food and Rural Affairs (DEFRA). In November 2018, XR organised a 'Rebellion Day' when thousands of people took part in a co-ordinated action to block the five main bridges over the Thames. Later that month, it oversaw a campaign known as 'swarming' roadblocks – repeated roadblocks of approximately seven minutes each – with small groups of activists occupying road junctions across London and blocking the roads around Parliament Square.

In January 2019, a Brighton section of the group organised a mass 'die-in' at a shopping centre that lasted for eleven minutes to represent the eleven years humanity had left to limit global warming to 1.5°C. They held banners about climate change and species extinction while a choir performed songs. The *Brighton Argus* newspaper reported that spectators applauded the protest.

The XR group has had unprecedented growth, support and media coverage across the UK. Its large-scale sit-ins and occupations have caused mass disruption, and this is a sure fire way to get your cause discussed. It also places pressure on those the protest is aimed at. However, those inconvenienced by the action may not always be sympathetic.

Letter campaigns and petitions

Not all protests require a physical presence; harnessing supporters who are geographically separated can also prove effective. This opens up your campaign to a wider demographic. Letters of protest sent en masse to a newspaper, institution, corporation or elected official can be an effective way to express your opinions and the concerns of a sector of the population. Well-written, clear and concise letters are more likely to be effective, and email delivery now enables fast, efficient communication, meaning many more people can be notified about and involved in a campaign.

Letter campaigns (including those using postcards and emails) work best if they are well thought out. They should be directed to someone who has the power to actually make the proposed change. The letters should also clearly state what action is required – for example, a change in legislation – and a date it should be achieved by. A large volume of letters can demonstrate how strongly people feel about the subject. Each year during November and December, Amnesty International runs its Write for Rights campaign, which encourages people to write messages of support to people around the world who have suffered injustice, and to become involved in the campaigns to help them. Many political prisoners have been released as a result, including Mexican torture victim Yecenia Armenta, and Albert Woodfox, who had been in solitary confinement in the USA.

Online petitions share some of the advantages of a letter campaign. They are accessible to many, they are cheap and they can attract a large number of supporters, without requiring those supporters to give up time usually spent with friends and family or at work. There's also the added bonus that if a petition from the UK Government's site attracts over 10,000 signatures, the Government has pledged it will respond. However, they also share a disadvantage with letter campaigns in that there is no physical presence, no massive inconvenience and thus sometimes little impact – and certainly no photo opportunity – for the media to share. The next chapter contains more information about online petitions and the success that can be achieved using them.

Strikes and go-slows

Some protests take place within the private sector. Industrial action campaigns can use the tactic of strikes, with employees refusing en masse to carry out their work. Campaigns may also use a deliberate delaying or slowing of work or progress (a go-slow). The disruption to services – and to profits – is always noticeable and can help apply pressure to the management.

Industrial action affects a wide range of workplaces. Recent examples include the rail industry, where workers have fought the removal of guards from trains; the education system, with teachers protesting funding cuts; and the health sector, where NHS staff have conducted walkouts to protest privatisation. At times, unionised industries also strike in support of other sectors. Figures released by the National Office for Statistics show that there were

276,000 working days lost due to labour disputes in the UK in 2017, the sixth-lowest annual total since records began in 1891.

Other actions

Of course, there are many other types of protests, including boycotts, emigration movements, the use of flash mobs, small-scale meetings in village halls and community centres, leafleting, lobbying, hacking, graffiti art and sabotage.

See you in court!

Another method of protest is to take out a civil action and let a court decide who is in the wrong. Legal test cases can be incredibly powerful and this practice of using the law within a campaign is sometimes referred to as 'judicial activism'. In May 2019, universal credit regulations were ruled unlawful[5] by the High Court following a case brought by individuals represented by legal firm Leigh Day and the Central England Law Centre. The claimants had argued that the regulations, which restrict the amount of compensation to those affected, were discriminatory.

However, legal challenges to Brexit have had mixed results; the attempt by the group called 'UK in EU Challenge' had asked the High Court to annul the result of the Brexit referendum on the grounds that the Leave campaign breached spending limits, and that the PM had failed to act on the growing evidence of illegality after investigations by the Electoral Commission.

The Brexit vote was also examined by the European Court of Justice (ECJ) after Jolyon Maugham QC of The Good Law Project launched the crowd-funded 'People's Challenge'. The campaign raised over £300,000 to challenge the Government's position that Article 50 could be triggered by Royal Prerogative. The ECJ ruled that the UK could cancel Brexit by unilaterally

[5] https://www.theguardian.com/society/2019/may/03/universal-credit-discrepancies-ruled-unlawful-by-high-court

revoking Article 50. In continued legal wrangles, Lord Trimble, the architect of the Good Friday Agreement, plans to take the Government to court over the 'backstop' in the Brexit Withdrawal Agreement. Eurotunnel also took legal action over the business impact of Brexit and, in March 2019, the Government agreed to pay £33m to settle a lawsuit over extra ferry services in the event of a no-deal Brexit.

Individuals can use the legal system to take a stand, too. In 2019, John Catt, a 94-year-old peaceful protestor, won an eight-year-long battle to force the police to delete details of his political activities from their database. Catt won his case in the European Court of Human Rights, where eight judges decided that the police had violated his human rights by retaining information about him – including descriptions of his appearance, clothes and his sketches drawn at demonstrations. Campaigners cite the case, demanding that the police close similar databases of protestors.

The sky's the limit
Everyday people are increasingly finding creative ways to get their points across – such as the funds raised for the inflatable 'Baby Trump' flown over Parliament Square when the President visited the UK in July 2018. The Trump blimp went on tour after the original protest, visiting Edinburgh and Paris. It also greeted Trump in Buenos Aires at the G20 summit and has continued to follow the president as the campaigners spent the £40,000-plus they raised for the balloon. Trump's daughter Ivanka was similarly targeted via a controversial art exhibition in Washington, with an installation that consists of a lookalike of her vacuuming and encourages visitors to toss crumbs for her to clean up.

Back in the UK, another innovative campaign calling itself 'Led by Donkeys' posted damning Twitter quotes by leading Brexiteers on billboards around the country. When Dominic Raab posted a tweet that suggested he hadn't understood the importance of the crossing to Calais from Dover, his tweet was pasted on a hoarding in the seaside town itself for all to see!

Another sure-fire way to garner publicity is to protest naked. Each year, the World Naked Bike Ride in London – it takes place in June, in case you need to clear your diary – sees scores of nude cycling fans take to the roads to protest car culture. Protesters also stripped to their underwear outside Victoria's Secret on Oxford Street to raise awareness of the lack of diversity representation in the fashion industry.

Another common theme is to organise protests at significant locations or on specific dates, such as an anniversary. On the seventieth anniversary of the National Health Service, locations across London saw activists drawing attention to healthcare cuts in recent years and the move to privatise parts of the service.

Final word

Many protests are often criticised for being ineffective because they don't stop wars or change government policies. But, while not every protest can perform a miracle, every single one of them brings the attention of new people to the cause, spreads awareness and makes politicians and other stakeholders think about which view they want to take (even if only to get more votes!). And while some acts might not have direct, quantifiable results, they are 100 per cent worthwhile, because activism is more often a marathon, not a sprint!

Case Study – Emily Lawrence

Wildlife campaigner Emily Lawrence was part of the organisational team responsible for a 2019 London march to the Japanese Embassy in protest of Japan's announcement that it intended to leave the International Whaling Commission (IWC). The direct action was designed to show that people in the UK were against the Japanese decision to resume commercial whaling along its country's north-east coasts for the first time in three decades. A letter to voice the concerns was also delivered to the embassy at the end of the demonstration.

Emily, whose responsibilities included planning the route, acting as police contact and running the event page on social media, says, 'If you feel something is not being taken seriously or you aren't being listened to, then direct action can be effective.' She believes petitions and marches are effective direct actions, explaining that these sorts of protests both create awareness and apply pressure to the government/council/group responsible to take action. The anti-whaling march was especially effective because Tokyo is due to host the Olympics in 2020 and is therefore on the international radar.

One of the concerns with Japan leaving the IWC was that it could set a dangerous precedent for other countries, such as South Korea and China, to follow. The idea behind the action in London was also to encourage a global movement, hopefully encouraging similar protests in other locations – including the USA, Australia and Canada – thereby generating huge public and political opposition to encourage the Japanese Government to change its mind.

To publicise actions like the London march, Emily recommends using social media, trying to get some press attention beforehand and asking non-governmental organisations (NGOs) if they can share the details to their supporters. Emily says that social media is a very important part of getting the word out there and helps to mobilise the public. But it is also important to create an action that the public can realistically take part in, and also to offer other ways to become involved – such as by sharing pictures and tweeting using a strong hashtag.

Emily agrees that apathy can be a problem, especially with issues such as Brexit on the agenda, but believes that British people do care and are prepared to fight for what they believe in. The important thing is to find a way to motivate them and ensure that they feel that they have made a meaningful difference by taking part. A direct action, such as a march, also brings people together for the same cause, explains Emily, and 'can lead to spin off groups and further actions by different groups or individuals'.

The march was bolstered by other campaign work, too, which included individuals emailing and writing to the embassy, or making the decision to boycott certain items. Emily's campaign also supports work by similar organisations, charities such as Sea Shepherd and the Dolphin project.

Takeaways

- Direct action can create awareness and apply pressure to decision-makers
- Target your activism by using a relevant location or significant time to have maximum impact
- Publicise your event via traditional and social media, and enlist the help of NGOs that share your agenda
- When you plan your action, ensure as many people as possible can participate; make the date, time and location suitable for as many people as possible
- Encourage those who cannot attend in person to support in other ways, by sharing a hashtag on social media, for example
- Remember the action should be just one part of your campaign, and can work to attract new supporters to your cause

9

Online Petitions

An online petition (or Internet petition or e-petition) is signed online, usually through a form on a website. They are free of charge and easy to set up and, once the required number of signatures is reached, the full petition is delivered to its target. Petitions have always been a useful tool for the activist but now their effectiveness has been given extra potency with the power of social media and improved global communications.

Change.org is the world's largest petition platform; it has around 200 million users in 196 countries, with more than 15 million of those in the UK. Another petition platform – the people-led 38 Degrees – has a community of over 3 million members and anyone can start a campaign, with those that gather the most momentum receiving support from the organisation's in-house team. At 38 Degrees, members choose which campaigns to support by voting in polls. The organisation also works offline, visiting MPs or ministers, running ads in the media, fundraising for legal action and holding meetings. Members of 38 Degrees have even descended on Parliament Square dressed as beekeepers and camped out in public toilets to promote the causes it supports.

The UK Government has its own system at www.gov.uk/petition-government, which has hosted more than 25,000 petitions. When a petition gathers more than 10,000 signatures, a response from the Government is promised; after reaching 100,000 signatures, petitions are considered for debate in Parliament. In January 2019, Newstalk.com reported that 266 petitions had received an official response from the gov.uk petition site, with 49 debated in the House of Commons.

In March 2019, the system notoriously crashed as the petition by Margaret Georgiadou to cancel Brexit went viral and trended on Twitter.

Success stories

Launched in 2009, and named after the tipping point when snow becomes an avalanche, 38 Degrees and its members have had several high-profile victories. These include:

- Stopping a Government sell-off of ancient national forests
- Scuppering plans for a mega-dairy in Lincolnshire
- Preventing Donald Trump's golf course expansion in Menie, Scotland
- Convincing the Government to sign an EU Directive on human trafficking
- Forcing 2012 Olympic sponsors to pay tax
- Stopping the sale of illegal bee-killing pesticides on eBay
- Preventing the hospital closure clause from becoming law

Submissions to the Government petition site have seen MPs debate a later start for secondary schools to increase productivity among teenagers as well as a call to lower the age for cervical smear tests. More than 10,000 people have also signed a petition started by the mother of Martyn Hett, who was among twenty-two people killed outside an Ariana Grande concert in May 2017, which calls on the Government to back better security at large public venues.

The Change.org platform also has plenty of notable success stories, and reports that nearly every hour a petition of Change.org achieves victory. Campaigns that have made a difference include one that called on Tesco to end the sale of eggs from caged hens[6]; another saw the Treasury vow to axe the 'tampon tax'[7]; and one

[6] https://www.telegraph.co.uk/women/life/meet-the-14-year-old-girl-who-convinced-tesco-bosses-to-stop-sel/
[7] https://www.theguardian.com/money/2016/mar/18/tampon-tax-scrapped-announces-osborne

petition successfully saw a young adult being moved from a Psychiatric Intensive Care Unit to a more appropriate specialist autism unit[8].

Penning successful petitions

Correct wording and structure will increase the chances of your petition becoming popular – the guidelines are not unlike those you might use for any campaign. To begin with, you need to consider your goal – choose one that is achievable and has a specific outcome. Rather than ask for a whole load of things, stick to one clear demand. Next, find out to whom the petition should be addressed. Again, be specific and find the person who really can make change happen. Addressing your petition to a single person is considered more effective.

Next, work on a catchy title – something that is short and easy to understand. You can include a specific location if that is applicable. You'll also need a few short lines that deftly summarise what you want to achieve and a longer description further down the page. Try to communicate why people should sign; outline the problem and what you want to do about it. Use real stories to illustrate the issue and add persuasive, well-sourced facts and figures. Make it personal and show you care. You can also use photos and videos to add interest and engage the audience.

Bolster your campaign

You can support your campaign by sharing on social media and encouraging others to do the same. Emailing your friends and family is a good place to start. Keep your petition page updated with any positive news, such as when you reach a large number of signatures, or if you make the news; this helps build momentum. You can also drum up support in the real world by running events, appearing in the media and asking people on the street to sign.

[8] https://www.bbc.co.uk/news/uk-england-london-35739304

Ultimately, you'll want to deliver your petition to your targeted individual. Consider how to make an impact when you do this. Delivering a petition at a council meeting is a popular option, or outside an office or an embassy. Invite the media and lots of your supporters, too. Prepare a simple speech and be polite so that you are taken seriously. You can repeat this process as your petition continues to grow or if there are new developments. There's no rule to say you can only hand over your petition once! This is not the end point either; keep following up on your petition, keeping your supporters in the loop. Celebrate a win publicly but, if you don't achieve what you want at the first attempt, keep going!

Petitioning Parliament

Any British citizen or UK resident can create or sign a petition that asks for a change to the law or to Government policy using the Government site. There are some rules, however, which are worth noting. A petition on the Government platform can only be considered if it asks about something that Parliament or the Government is actually responsible for; the subject cannot be something that's the responsibility of the Scottish Parliament or Welsh Assembly. Any petitions that cover legal cases active in the UK courts or that name people working in public bodies (except for senior management) are also not accepted.

On the Government site, once you have created a petition, you will be guided on how to get five people to support it. It is checked and then published. Those that do not meet the standards outlined above are rejected. The Petitions Committee reviews all petitions and it has the power to press for action from Government or Parliament. At 10,000 signatures, you will receive a response from the Government, while at 100,000 signatures your petition will be considered for a debate in Parliament unless the issue has been debated recently or is already scheduled. Some petitions may be debated before they reach 100,000 signatures. Individuals behind a petition that is to be debated may well be contacted for further information and/or invited to discuss the issue with MPs or a committee.

Online petitions – the positives

An online petition offers a fast track to campaigning. Setting one up takes minutes and signing them can be even quicker. They also have an incredible reach and influence, with a sympathetic audience already built in. While, for a time, it could be argued that online petitions were open to misuse, the platforms now take signature verification very seriously, employing safeguards such as confirmation emails and proof of identity, as you would in the real world. They are now considered robust and fit for purpose.

Online petitions – the downside

The 'e-protest' movement has plenty of dissenters – with frequent accusations of 'slacktivism' – a pejorative term suggesting that signing an online petition is simply an ineffective measure that the public carries out to feel good about themselves, and that those people rarely go any further out of their way to support an issue.

Commentators have also analysed those petitions garnering the most signatures on the Government site and the effect the petitions went on to have. A prime example of this is the petition to stop Donald Trump's state visit to the UK, the third-most signed online campaign in the history of Parliament's site. More than a million people signed the petition, but Downing Street dismissed the idea. The Government also rejected a request to trigger a second Brexit referendum if either vote won less than 60 per cent based on a turnout of less than 75 per cent. The Government also rejected calls to extend the Meningitis B vaccination programme to *all* children – not just newborn babies – despite 823,348 members of the public signing a petition requesting it.

Other popular petitions that failed to achieve their desired result include one that asked for Trump to be denied access to the UK; another that demanded all immigration be stopped and UK borders closed until Isis was defeated; a request for a vote of 'No Confidence' in Jeremy Hunt, Health Secretary; and a call to legalise the production, sale and use of cannabis.

However, one petition arguing that the UK should offer proportional asylum in comparison with European counterparts did have some success, with the then-PM David Cameron confirming 20,000 more Syrians would be resettled under the Syrian Vulnerable Persons Relocation (VPR) scheme and a further £100m would be spent in humanitarian aid.

More than just signatures

While figures showing the success or failure of highly-publicised petitions make for a good story, it's deceptive to suggest that they don't have any impact at all. It isn't always possible to trace a direct, quantifiable change in law or policy from an online petition, but those petitions that have millions of signatures send a powerful message about what the public wants and believes in.

Case Study – Rebecca Atkinson

#ToyLikeMe was established in April 2015 after journalist Rebecca Atkinson decided to tackle the lack of positive representation of diversity in toys. Rebecca grew up wearing hearing aids, and knew first-hand how it felt to be a child who never saw themselves represented by mainstream toys. She believes this lack of inclusivity in play teaches children it's OK to exclude people in real life. Her aim was to get global brands like Lego, Mattel and Playmobil to include positive representations of disability in their products – though it is worth noting that #ToyLikeMe uses the term 'diff:ability' to cover all aspects of difference from birthmarks to prosthetic limbs.

Rebecca began giving toys makeovers in order to reflect a range of differences. She took high-res images and shared them online. The results went viral and #ToyLikeMe found itself featured in the media the world over.

After making-over Playmobil figures with guide dogs and wheelchairs, Rebecca started a Change.org petition asking Playmobil to produce the figures for real; over 50,000 people signed and Playmobil agreed to do it. A further Change.org petition called on Lego to follow suit, but despite over 20,000 people signing, Lego didn't respond. Undeterred, #ToyLikeMe launched a wheelchair Father Christmas on the Lego Ideas platform. Eventually, in January 2016, Lego unveiled their first ever wheelchair-using mini-figure, with the UK press attributing the move to Rebecca's campaign[9].

In February 2016, #ToyLikeMe gave a batch of Tinkerbell dolls some hot pink cochlear implants and took some snaps, gaining more publicity and, by the summer, it had launched a website backed with £17,000 raised through crowdfunding. The website shares products that represent diversity and responds to every single email it receives from parents looking for a toy that embodies a particular difference.

The organisation now collaborates with the Lottie Dolls brand to produce the world's first doll with a cochlear implant, which proudly carries the 'Loved by #ToyLikeMe' endorsement. #ToyLikeMe has evolved to become a successful arts and play not-for-profit, and alongside its makeovers of example toys designed to

[9] https://www.theguardian.com/culture/2016/jan/27/lego-unveils-disabled-minifigure-promobricks-nuremberg-toy-fair

encourage the industry to produce their own, it also offers workshops to teach inclusion and diversity to primary schools.

#ToyLikeMe's first Change.org petition was the result of an article about the company that appeared in the *Guardian*, when Change.org encouraged Rebecca to use its platform, supporting her with advice along the way. Rebecca believes its success was a response to the strong and novel idea of #ToyLikeMe and that the online nature of her campaign works particularly because 'disabled people are scattered around the world, meaning there are millions worldwide but only a minority in each small town'. Online campaigning allowed Rebecca to reach an international disabled network, amassing numbers in a way that local campaigning never would.

The rapid success of #ToyLikeMe's Change.org petition was also partly due to Change.org promoting the petition directly to those on its database it thought would be interested, says Rebecca. This allowed her to continue to update signees, and to have access to a group of supporters that she wouldn't otherwise have been able to reach.

Some of these supporters have gone on to help fund the development of #ToyLikeMe. The impact of Rebecca's online petitions has gone beyond just demonstrating to the industry the need and demand for inclusive toys, but also in raising money for Rebecca's work to continue.

Not surprisingly, Rebecca's top tip for online petitioning is to 'get Change.org on board', and although she accepts it can't back every petition, she believes if it chooses to support yours, it's likely to be successful.

Takeaways

- Petitions have always been important in campaigning, with online petitions reducing costs and manpower
- Online campaigning can help you reach geographically diverse supporters
- The popularity of an online petition can have many positive results, including press attention, a boost in fundraising, the backing of the petition host site itself and even participation in how a change is made or legislated
- Keeping in touch with those who have signed your petition is essential, so remember to keep your petition news updated and encourage your supporters to follow you on social media, too

10

Pressure Groups

A pressure group is an organisation set up to influence both public opinion and authorities such as the Government, often in an attempt to change laws or regulations at a local, national or international level. The organisation will look to exert pressure on legislators and challenge beliefs to promote their own aims. There are many pressure groups in the UK and throughout the world, covering topics as varied as animal welfare and the environment to business and LGBTQ+ rights.

Typically, a pressure group will have a narrow or single issue it focuses and campaigns on, and employs tactics such as letter writing, marches and other events, looking to place coverage of its work in the media. A pressure group often has cross-party support, rather than being aligned to one political party. Some groups will be well known to the public because of their use of celebrity ambassadors or because of direct action and publicity stunts. Father's rights organisation Fathers4Justice, for example, often hit headlines for acts such as storming on to live TV, defacing works of art and climbing public buildings dressed as superheroes. Greenpeace has, in the past, commissioned a giant mechanical polar bear to walk the streets of London, had members scale Nelson's Column and produced the short 'Rang-tan' animation supermarket brand Iceland used in its since-banned Christmas ad in 2018.

Charities, trade unions, churches and professional associations also come under the category of pressure groups, providing services and lobbying the Government. They are often referred to as 'interest' or 'special interest' groups, an example of which is the British Medical Association (BMA) and the National

Farmers' Union (NFU). Such groups may have a closed membership. The term 'cause group' is also used to describe organisations made up of people who share the same attitudes and beliefs around a certain subject, examples of which include the Royal Society for the Prevention of Cruelty to Animals (RSPCA) and Shelter. You may also hear about international pressure groups such as the Red Cross referred to as 'non-governmental organisations' (NGOs).

Inside or outside?

Pressure groups are further divided into those that work closely with the Government, the 'insider' groups, and those that don't, which are known as 'outsider' groups. Insider groups are regularly consulted by the Government, perhaps sitting on policy or parliamentary committees, and may prove to be more influential. Here, too, there are some distinctions, with groups operating at low- or high-profile level, or as an 'ultra-insider', having a large public and political presence, and being regularly consulted by Government ministers.

Outsider groups may instead focus on influencing policy via public support or through the media. Again, not all outsider groups are the same – some will be seeking to become insiders, others may remain outsiders because they lack the resources to become insiders, while other groups do not want to work with the establishment. The Campaign for Nuclear Disarmament – CND – is an example of a group that feels its integrity might be compromised by too close an association with the Government. These types of groups are more likely to employ strategies such as petitions, demos and civil disobedience.

How do they work?

Pressure groups can be highly effective when they have the attention of ministers and civil servants, and if they are consulted regularly. Those within pressure groups are useful to the authorities because they often have both specialist knowledge and a feel for how the community as a whole will respond to relevant legislation. They can provide valuable input and advice as new laws are formed. Pressure groups will also work to educate MPs and the public through their work.

Apart from pressure groups, the only other way to influence government decisions directly is through one of the political parties, so clearly pressure groups are incredibly important in advocating change. Interestingly, membership and public interest in these groups is also increasing, while satisfaction with the main political parties seems to be decreasing, with low voter turnout and increased participation in activism, such as protest marches.

Examples of pressure groups include Greenpeace, Sustain, the World Wide Fund for Nature (WWF) and Shelter. Groups such as these can help you by providing information, research and guidance. You can learn from their campaigns and, in some cases, take an active part in their work, too.

All groups large and small

While some pressure groups have an overall mission and campaign on the smaller issues within that arena, other groups form to deal with specific concerns. The UK-based pressure group Windrush Movement, for example, is currently working to ensure greater transparency and assurances from the Jamaican Government following the Windrush scandal, which saw the British Government deport Jamaicans from the UK despite those affected having the right of abode. The group is also monitoring compensation arrangements for those affected.

Case Study – Niall Couper, Amnesty

Amnesty is a campaigning organisation that 'gives a voice to the voiceless' and shines a light on human rights concerns that are otherwise hidden from public view. It began campaigning in 1961 but has grown from seeking the release of political prisoners to covering a whole spectrum of issues including sexual and reproductive rights, torture, the use of the death penalty, discrimination and the rights of refugees and migrants.

Amnesty achieves its goals through a wide-range of activities include raising awareness, lobbying, using the media and social media, and organising local events. Each method is chosen based on its suitability and effectiveness for that concern at the time. Niall Couper, Head of Media, PR and Supporter Communications at the organisation, says, 'Without such groups as Amnesty, there is no one to hold people to account for their actions.'

One of Amnesty's most significant successes is the creation of an Arms Trade Treaty, says Niall, although the day-to-day work of speaking up for those who can't and helping to free individuals at risk can't be underplayed. Despite its success in many areas, there are still plenty of battles to be won. The ultimate success would be the absence of a need for Amnesty any longer, explains Niall.

Since Amnesty is a member-led organisation, the individuals that support it 'are essential to us' says Niall. He explains that it is easy to get involved, either by joining one of Amnesty's youth, local or student groups; or by getting involved with one of its many networks. Amnesty has specialist networks that cover Trade Unions, the rights of women, children and LGBTQ+ individuals, and a network for teachers interested in bringing human rights into their classroom. 'You could take an action and show your support for one of the many cases we work on around the world. The Amnesty website has full details of ongoing campaigns. You can also volunteer,' he says.

Amnesty has several self-help guides available through its website[10] that give you tips on how to campaign, ideas for activities you could do locally – either as a group or an individual – and even how to conduct a media interview.

Individual activists are considered 'the bread and butter of our organisation' says Niall, and that 'without them, Amnesty is powerless'. He also has some words of motivation for people unhappy with the way the world works, explaining that it's always worth being active in bringing change. He says, 'If you do nothing, nothing will happen. Only by action can you play a part in making the world a better place. You can't leave it all up to someone else.'

Takeaways

- Large pressure groups often already have the attention of the Government department you hope to influence
- Consider joining forces with a pressure group that shares your campaign goals
- Pressure groups value the opinions of and the work that members offer
- Check the websites of pressure groups; they may offer materials and guides that can be of practical use to you
- Don't hold back! Join in and make a difference!

---

[10] www.amnesty.org.uk/key-resources-local-groups

All-Party Parliamentary Groups

All-Party Parliamentary Groups (APPGs) are informal cross-party groups that have no official status within Parliament. They are run by and for Members of the Commons and Lords, though many choose to involve individuals and organisations from outside Parliament in their administration and activities.

The groups discuss and monitor a particular country, industry, social issue or area of concern. To be called an APPG, the group must be open to all members of both Houses, regardless of party affiliation. The groups provide a valuable opportunity for parliamentarians to engage with those outside Parliament and vice versa.

The parliamentary website[11] maintains an APPG register listing all of the groups, which is regularly updated and published online approximately every six weeks. The list shows the title and the purpose of the group, its officers and full contact details, as well as providing details of annual general meetings (AGMs) and any monetary benefits, or benefits in kind, the group receives. Some of the groups represent a particular country or industry, with the aim of developing beneficial relationships and policies. Other groups centre on particular subjects, which can include illnesses and issues such as ageing, LGBTQ+ rights, ocean conservation, race, electoral reform, refugees, single-parent families and women in the workplace. Rumour has it that the Chair of the APPG for Beer and Pubs was known informally for some years as the Minister for Fun!

APPGs must abide by certain rules, which are also displayed online. The rules mostly relate to membership, meetings,

[11] www.parliament.uk

publications and the finances of each group. The key requirements are making and maintaining a Register entry, admitting members and electing officers, holding meetings and maintaining transparency. The groups should not be confused with Select Committees, which are also a cross-party group of MPs or Lords. Select Committees, however, have been given a specific remit to investigate and report back to the House, and the Government must respond to their findings.

Why do they matter?

Typically, an APPG exists to influence – and potentially challenge and change – Government policy. They may publish research, offer expertise or run inquiries. Forming and chairing an APPG can be an effective way to campaign within and to influence Parliament, helping MPs sympathetic to your cause to spread awareness and use the group and its events to generate publicity. It's virtually the only way to reach a wide spectrum of MPs at once, since the nature of a cross-party group means that politicians from both sides of the House attend.

Encouraging an MP to form an APPG could give your campaign a massive boost if a central part of your mission is to change the law or introduce a new one. Be prepared to offer to help with any organisational and administrative tasks that need to be done to get the group up and running and maintain it. The formation of a new group requires four MPs and peers, from opposition and Government parties. If you want to recruit other interested MPs to beef up the group and further increase your reach, you can research via the *Hansard* website[12], which keeps a record of all parliamentary debates. TheyWorkForYou[13] offers a keyword search of parliamentary debates dating back to the 1930s!

If suitable APPGs already exist, working with them is a great

[12] hansard.parliament.uk
[13] www.theyworkforyou.com

way to increase the visibility of your issue, and to connect and build relationships with parliamentarians and others who may be willing to support your cause. Make yourself indispensable to the APPG by offering assistance, attending meetings and publicising the work of the group. Make the most of your personal experience on the issue, and ask if you may speak at the next meeting to share your first-hand knowledge. This is your chance to inspire MPs concerned with the issues you raise to ask questions in the House and lobby on your behalf.

To get in touch with an existing group, check the Register via the Parliament site for a point of contact. You could also consider asking your local MP to attend an upcoming meeting of an APPG. This would be particularly helpful if the issues that will be discussed affect their constituency.

When you plan to attend an APPG meeting, leave plenty of time to get through the security checks at the entrance of the parliamentary buildings as the queues build up, and take some photo ID with you in case you are asked to show it.

Case Study – APDAWG

The All-Party Parliamentary Dogs Advisory Welfare Group (APDAWG) was set up in 2017 to explore, highlight, discuss and challenge dog-related activities, legislation and trends with the overall aim of improving the health and welfare of the UK's dogs and dog owners, and society in general.

Dr Lisa Cameron MP acts as the group's Chair, with co-founder Marc Abraham as Secretariat. At the time of the #LucysLaw campaign, the cross-party MPs appointed as Vice-Chairs included Zac Goldsmith, John McNally, Andrea Jenkyns, Ross Thompson, Tommy Sheppard, Ann Clwyd and Chris Williamson.

APDAWG works closely with the Association of Lawyers for Animal Welfare (ALAW) and is attended by campaigners, organisations and individuals keen to improve canine welfare.

The APDAWG holds regular informal meetings that feature an expert panel and encourage discussion on topics such as the use of electric collars, pet theft reform, the use of dogs in animal experiments, unsung heroes in the dog arena and the links between dog fighting and animal cruelty to domestic violence.

APDAWG's inaugural meeting discussed the immediate ban of third-party puppy sales. The Dogs Trust, Blue Cross and Battersea Dogs & Cats Home were invited to explain why they refused to support such a ban. APDAWG played an integral role in securing the new legislation, which became known as #LucysLaw, that ended third-party puppy sales. Other successful campaigns that APDAWG has supported and/or spearheaded include Finn's Law, which sought to secure protection for Britain's service dogs, and was named after a police dog that was stabbed while working. This new law came into force in June 2019, and saw service animals treated as sentient beings under law rather than just as items of property. This means that those harming a service animal can be charged under the Animal Welfare Act 2006 and cannot use the defence of fear to excuse suffering inflicted upon the animal.

Lisa says it's a 'pleasure and a privilege' to be the Chair of such a well-supported group, and that secretariat Marc has gone 'above and beyond' to support the group and 'to ensure it gives a voice and campaigns for dog welfare issues'. She also says that APDAWG is one of the busiest APPGs in Parliament, and has had an unprecedented level of success in a short time, including the formation of a similar group for the protection of cats. It receives extensive support not just from the people who attend but also from those who link up with the group online and on social media to support the campaigns. In fact, the meetings are often packed out – even in the largest of the meeting rooms Parliament has to offer.

Lisa believes the group is popular because Britain really is a nation of animal lovers, and that the public sympathises with any injustice that affects vulnerable animals as they can't speak up for themselves. APDAWG is the voice for those animals in Parliament, she explains. She now looks forward to supporting campaigns that seek harsher sentences for animal cruelty and closing the loophole on dog meat consumption in the UK – while our current laws prohibit taking a dog to a slaughterhouse, in theory you can kill and eat your own dog if the slaughter is undertaken 'humanely'; Lisa believes we should show leadership on this topic internationally. The group is also working on improving the welfare of greyhounds, some of which are currently being exported to China and end up in the dog meat market there.

Takeaways

- All-Party Parliamentary Groups target specialist interests
- Anyone can ask to join an existing group and become involved
- Expect cross-party politicians and relevant charities and NGOs to attend, alongside interested members of the public
- APPGs hold meetings in the Houses of Parliament, so bring photo ID and leave plenty of time to allow for security checks before you arrive
- APPGs are the best way to reach a wide spectrum of MPs simultaneously
- If you can't find a fit for your campaign, consider creating a new APPG with a sympathetic MP

12

The Media

The term 'the media' can be all encompassing – with overlapping and interchangeable phrases such as 'news media' and 'mass media' often bandied about by those within the industry. However, in terms of widening the reach of a campaign, the media you need to concentrate on working with are any communication channels that can share your message with others. In a practical sense, this means printed and digital newspapers, magazines, books, radio and TV channels, and online content outlets such as podcasts. These are the channels that are responsible for sharing news, entertainment, education, information and promotional messages with the public.

What can the media do for you?

Many an amateur philosopher has found themselves musing upon the question, 'If a tree falls in a forest and no one is around to hear it, does it make a sound?' Likewise, you should ask, 'If your campaign isn't getting the attention it deserves, is it making a difference?' Media coverage can be essential to the success of an activist.

Think of the media as a 'multiplier' in the sense that the more people who learn about your campaign, the bigger the impact becomes. And the bigger the impact you have, the more people will learn about your campaign! The publishing and broadcasting industries can help you get your message and/or your story out to the widest audience. And it's free of charge – essential for a campaign operating on a voluntary basis with no financial backing, which, let's face it, most of them are.

The media will help you target your message, too, because it is hugely varied and has many niches to exploit, one of which will be just the right audience for your needs. Appearing within the media will both bolster your support and add a sense of legitimacy to your group because, generally, the public respect and trust the outlets they choose to listen to, view or read. This credibility also extends to the decision-makers and stakeholders you are aiming to influence. Ultimately, an attentive media audience is more likely to support you after hearing positive coverage.

But, while your group won't have to pay for media coverage, there will be a certain amount of work you will need to do in order to give yourself the best chance of obtaining it. Invest time in building relationships with the media (part of the PR tools covered in Chapter 7), have information and releases ready and offer a reliable and coherent spokesperson.

Which is the right publication for you?

There are thousands of media opportunities out there; the trick is deciding which ones to target. The media outlets your campaign could feature on include:

- Local radio
- Local TV
- National radio
- National TV
- National newspapers (and their online counterparts)
- Local newspapers (and their online counterparts)
- National magazines (trade, consumer and customer)
- Local magazines/guides
- Online-only publications
- Podcasts
- Blogs (both personal and those that are published by a larger media outlet, e.g. the *Huffington Post*)

So how do you decide which ones are for you?

Local or national?

Perhaps your first question might be to ask if coverage of your campaign is a local or a national story? The truth is, of course, is that it can be both, depending entirely on how you frame it (more on that later). However, when you approach the media, you must remember that each outlet will only run stories that suit its target audience. Therefore, a local outlet will focus only on stories that are relevant to the local audience, asking how this affects the immediate community. Usual topics include local sport, crime, business, events and politics. Does your story have a local angle? The angle might exist because you are a local resident, or because a fundraising event is happening in the area or it could be the local impact of a national policy or event.

A national media outlet, however, has a broader readership and therefore a wider range of content, including international news and events. Ask yourself if people outside your town or city are likely to care about your campaign, or if you can link it to a wider issue that does affect people across the country. Alternatively, do you have some kind of hook – perhaps something never seen or done before, or something truly unusual, provocative or outrageous that might warrant national interest? Those naked bike rides against car culture always get national coverage!

Newspaper or magazine?

So, is your story right for a newspaper or a magazine? Well, if it is time-sensitive – meaning it reacts to an event or situation that is current and likely to change – then its natural home is definitely a newspaper, where coverage tends to be shorter, too (300-500 words for a paper, around 2,000 for a magazine article).

Stories or features within magazines have no such restrictions. Features also tend to have more space and time to include case studies – and these are a great way to introduce a 'real' person affected by the issue you are campaigning about – and make an impact. It's worth bearing in mind, though, that some sections of some larger newspapers, such as weekend papers, also work in the same way as magazines.

Don't forget that the magazine market extends well beyond the consumer titles you see displayed on a shop shelf – what would usually be called newsstand publications or glossies – targeted at the general public. There are plenty of trade magazines, whose audience is made up of people who work in a particular trade or industry. Many businesses, such as John Lewis, Boots and ASDA, produce customer magazines, too. They tend to have the look and feel of a newsstand publication, but typically are paid for by the company rather than advertisers, with the aim of communicating with customers. It's likely you may also have some smaller local magazines in your area as well.

TV or radio?
Many TV chat shows prefer to feature people who have already appeared in the press, so it can be difficult to achieve this coverage. TV producers are likely to be interested in a topic if it is already popular and being talked about. Viewers are then interested to hear what the opposing views on the issue are, and to see people express their own opinions. If you are an expert on a certain topic, a TV chat show is a great way to further your cause. If your campaign has an investigative side, a documentary might also be an option. Again, case studies – people who have been personally affected by the topic that you are campaigning for – also make for good TV.

Radio has certain limitations – and that is mainly time and the way that listeners can be expected to absorb information they hear. Because the audience can't control the pace of radio, listeners will find facts and figures harder to understand, and they are easily forgotten. Radio is not the place for fact-heavy material or lengthy pieces.

Radio is often split along the lines of national and local press.

Again, regional stations are interested in issues that affect their immediate community, or a local angle on a nationwide story. National radio typically covers larger issues and interesting talking points, and it may also have a specific audience demographic, such as the age group it appeals to. A good national story should focus on an issue or a certain type of audience, while a local radio station will focus on its geographical region.

Online?

And don't forget there are also endless web options for your story, including online versions of publications, specific e-zines, blogs, YouTube and podcasts. And while each of these examples might have a particular focus, the general rule is that Internet content should be visual – both in terms of the availability of pictures and videos and in the way text is presented (broken up and easy to read). It's all too easy to scroll on by when online, so your content must be eye-catching and immediate.

And finally, bear in mind that the same story can be used in different outlets by changing the way it is presented to fit the desired format. While the facts stay the same, the angle and presentation will change to cater for the audience. You just need to find the right story to 'sell'.

How do I make my campaign media-friendly?

The media are generally interested in storytelling, which means that it looks for the real-life story behind an issue. This may take the form of a personal tragedy, a hobby that has grown into something bigger and made an impact, the way your campaign has changed someone's life or something quirky, like an organisation, building or item. Seek out the amazing or unusual to attract the media or offer your services as an expert commentator.

The hook

For many journalists, a story can't run unless it has a hook – a critical piece of newsworthy information that will grab the audience's attention. An example of a seasonal hook is a tie-in with events such as Christmas, Valentine's Day or Hallowe'en, while a news hook would peg your campaign to current headlines. Keep on top of the news and be ready to contact the press when your topic comes up. You might be able to use newly released survey data or statistics. Ask yourself why your story or the story of your campaign is unusual and significant enough to merit coverage by considering 'why this story ... why now?' Try and summarise your sell in a few lines and see how snappy it is.

Develop a relationship

Don't expect to be the media's first port of call if they've only just met you. A relationship with editors, writers and broadcasters will take time to nurture. Expect to have to prove that you can be relied on to provide relevant information to a deadline. Try to be very quick in reacting to breaking news and contact people straight away. Live TV and radio programmes are often tight on time when they need guests and contributors. If you have a preferred outlet, offer an exclusive.

Case studies to care about

If you're taking the human angle, you'll need strong named and pictured case studies, as audiences tend to engage more when they have a person to care about. People presenting their own case studies work best when the individuals featured are presentable and reflect the demographic of the audience – so it's worth having a mix of ages, genders, ethnicities and social backgrounds to offer. The case study individual will also need to be friendly, open and able to talk with emotion about the topic. They may have to be interviewed on the same topic several times over, so they need to be patient. It's also unlikely they will have copy approval when pieces are printed, so it's worth ensuring they are happy with this from the outset. Crucially, they will need to be flexible and readily available!

Making it easy

If you want to increase your chances of getting press coverage, make life easy for journalists and editors by providing something that can easily be lifted and used such as pull-out quotes and a ready-made headline. The same goes for images – offer them in a variety of resolutions and orientations so that they can be quickly fitted into space without any chasing. Remember to add details of the credit – this saves the picture editor another job. Having video available will also increase your chances with online outlets. For local issues, a well-attended demo or a popular petition will also help add interest. Take some time to work out different angles, and use those angles to pitch your idea to appropriate outlets. Be ready to go if there's a request for the case study individual to appear or be interviewed.

What not to do

It's important not to waste the time of professionals; don't bombard them with irrelevant information or self-promotion. Think in terms of the boy who cried wolf: if you send through information that's of no use all the time, when you do have something relevant they won't be listening! Check and check again that all of your case studies are happy to be used – there's nothing more frustrating than a last-minute change of heart and a gaping space in an article or broadcast.

When things go wrong

Having an established relationship with your local and national media can also help should you find yourself with any negative coverage, or when mistakes are made. If you are already well known for commenting on a topic, if you are happy to make yourself available and polite when an enquiry comes through, you are more likely to be contacted to provide balance for an article. If any criticism has been levelled at your campaign, it is essential to be ready to respond to it. However, if you feel you have been misrepresented in the media, or that the information published or broadcast was incorrect, you have several options.

The Independent Press Standards Organisation (IPSO) is the independent regulator for the newspaper and magazine industry in the UK. IPSO has a code of practice called The Editors' Code that it expects all members to follow, and it will investigate if it receives a complaint about a breach of these standards. IPSO has the power to make newspapers and magazines publish corrections or adjudications and can fine publishers up to £1 million. It also investigates media intrusion, offering a 24-hour emergency hotline for anyone who feels they are being harassed by journalists (office hours: 0300 123 22 20; out of hours; 07799 903 929).

Ofcom is the regulator for communications services, and regulates both TV and radio. Its Broadcasting Code contains rules broadcasters must follow; however, if your complaint is about BBC TV or radio programmes, or programmes watched on BBC iPlayer, you must use the BBC's own complaints system[14].

Complaining about inaccurate online content can be more difficult. Your first port of call is to complain to the website itself. If you are having trouble finding contact details, you can check the 'WHOIS' register, which should list the contact details for the registrar of a particular domain name, or direct you to their website. Every registered domain name should in theory have identifying contact information. The WHOIS database is operated by many registrars and registries, all monitored by The

---

[14] www.bbc.co.uk/complaints
[15] ICANN www.icann.org

Internet Corporation for Assigned Names and Numbers[15]. If you are unhappy with the progress you make, the Internet Services Providers' Association (ISPA UK), the UK's Trade Association for providers of Internet services, might also be able to help. If you believe the content breaks the law, then you can contact the police.

Case Study – Marc Abraham, #LucysLaw and the *Daily Mirror*

The #LucysLaw campaign called for a ban on the sale of puppies by pet shops and other third parties who are not the breeders. It was conceived by TV vet and PupAid founder Marc Abraham and named after a Cavalier King Charles spaniel rescued from a puppy farm in 2013.

Some areas of the puppy retail trade had been linked to unethical dog breeding for profit. Pet shops and online sites such as Gumtree provided an environment which was one step removed from the reality of those puppies' breeding and living conditions; they often came from high-volume, low-welfare puppy farms. Had those horrific environments been visible to the purchaser, it would undoubtedly have deterred many from buying these pets. Puppy farm puppies can have deadly infectious diseases such as parvovirus, congenital problems and long-term physical and emotional issues. The breeding parents at puppy farms endure years of neglect and over-breeding, and can be heartlessly disposed of once they can no longer produce puppies. They may never leave the cold, dark and dirty sheds they are kept in until they die. In some cases, dogs would barely have had human contact either, as the food and watering processes involve minimal effort. It's a miserable life, and a miserable end.

Marc invited the *Daily Mirror* to be the media partner of the #LucysLaw campaign because he was so impressed by a 'beautifully written and well-researched' article by investigative staff journalist Andrew Penman. His 2016 piece asked what puppy farmers had to hide after Penman was refused entry time and time again when he attempted to visit large-scale commercial dog breeders in Carmarthenshire and Ceredigion, which were well-known hubs for bulk breeders.

The Government advice for anyone thinking of buying a puppy had always been to see the dog with its mother, which is impossible if puppy farmers refuse to let you in and instead sell their dogs on to shops hundreds of miles away. A change in the law to ban third-party sales prevented puppy farmers from passing on their puppies to be sold elsewhere.

Teaming up with the *Daily Mirror* was 'pivotal to the success' of the campaign says Marc, and included the creation of a 'microsite' on the publication's website that effectively kept a chronological storyline of each article that covered #LucysLaw. For its part, the *Daily Mirror* fully embraced the demand for a change in the law, running a related piece each week, and providing other support by designing the campaign logo and other materials. Marc believes the *Daily Mirror* and its journalists were part of the success of #LucysLaw, and 'deserve all the recognition' for taking the initial risk in supporting the campaign and always prioritising the welfare of the dogs above ego, even retweeting coverage on the topic from rival titles and showing the cross-party political support it received.

The paper faced criticism of and potential legal action against its support of #LucysLaw, not least when it began to name and shame the organisations that would not support the ban on third-party sales.

A partnership with the *Daily Mirror* also offered access to a key demographic Marc needed to reach with his message, and an endorsement from a well-respected title gave the campaign credibility. The *Daily Mirror* also offered the advantage of having an online presence, too – ideal for sharing relevant stories and progress on social media – and has no pay wall to prevent access. Penman's articles were never politically divisive, despite the *Daily Mirror* typically being viewed as a left-wing newspaper. Its regular updates kept the campaign and the conversation about the ban in the public eye. Marc describes this constant dialogue as being like 'gold dust', and the media partnership as 'an amazing tool, a dream' for the campaign.

So, what did the #LucysLaw campaign offer for the *Daily Mirror* in return for its support? And does it tell us what the media wants from potential allies? Marc believes that the storytelling aspect perfectly suited the paper, and that every article was a continuing piece of the narrative, every success a piece of positive progress for those engaged with the story. Each week the audience could see the story unfold, and the *Daily Mirror* was able to take ownership of that and influence it, too. The relationship between the #LucysLaw campaign and the *Daily Mirror* was 'symbiotic' he explains – 'we gave them the content, they turned it into copy'.

Marc pays tribute to Andrew Penman, whom he describes as a 'decent, brave, investigative journalist', who always made time for #LucysLaw, and was generous with his time, writing phenomenal articles. 'I can never thank him enough,' he says.

And the outcome of all this co-ordinated effort? After years of campaigning, #LucysLaw will become law on 6 April 2020, imposing a ban on all commercial third-party sales of puppies and kittens. Breeders, who must be licensed, will therefore be required to sell direct to the public only animals they have bred – they must not pass those puppies or kittens on to a middle-man to trade. Buyers should then be able to assess fairly the conditions under which those animals were bred.

Takeaways

- Teaming up with the media offers great opportunities for a campaign to get its message across
- Regular pieces in mainstream media keep the story fresh in everyone's minds, creating a narrative of the campaign development
- Think about who you are trying to reach, and find a media outlet that is appropriate for that demographic
- Look for a story with a hook so journalists can feature your campaign
- Strong case studies help the audience engage with a story, make sure yours is media friendly
- Work to establish an ongoing relationship with your favoured outlets; this will lead to greater trust and more opportunities and support

Social Media

Activism has long existed in the public consciousness, but no one can deny how much the Internet and social media have increased the exposure of campaigners and their movements to significantly more people. Figures from We Are Social show the number of social media users worldwide in 2018 was 3.196 billion, up 13 per cent year-on-year. And harnessing the reach that platforms like Facebook and Twitter offer enables activists to organise protests large and small with high levels of engagement and focus. But why is this exactly?

Fast and friendly

Social media offers a massive boost to campaigns because it allows information to circulate quickly and freely. It originates within our own online network and therefore carries with it the same type of validation we attach to 'word of mouth' – put simply, we are likely to trust it, whether it comes from a friend, or a friend of a friend of a friend. Online networks also operate in real time and allow for an immediate response, meaning actions such as donations and petition signing can be acted on then and there, before the impetus is lost. The platforms also foster a level of involvement in social movements and events we might not otherwise feel.

There are a seemingly endless number of social media platforms you can use to publicise your campaign and encourage engagement. It's likely you'll be familiar with the main sites, such as Twitter, Facebook, Instagram, YouTube, Pinterest and LinkedIn, but how many more platforms can you name? Here are some you might not be familiar with – and a little summary of what they do:

- Flickr – an image and video hosting service
- Tumblr – a microblogging site
- Quora – a community question-and-answer website
- WhatsApp – a freeware and cross-platform messaging and voiceover IP service
- Snapchat – a multimedia messaging app
- Reddit – members submit content, which are then voted up or down by other members
- Foursquare – a local search-and-discovery mobile app
- MeetUp – organises online groups that host in-person events for people with similar interests
- Mix (formerly StumbleUpon) – allows you to curate and share Internet content
- Care2 – connects activists from around the world with individuals, organisations and responsible businesses
- NextDoor – a private social network for your neighbourhood community
- TikTok – an app for creating and sharing short videos

Which is best?

Of course, asking which social media platform is going to give your campaign the biggest boost is like asking about the proverbial piece of string. Some platforms are better suited to picture content (such as Flickr and Instagram), while others like Facebook, Twitter, Tumblr and Quora allow for varying amounts of text (although adding pictures or videos can still be important for engagement). In May 2019, YouGov ranked the most popular UK social networks as Facebook, Google+, Instagram and Twitter[16]. Facebook is also dominant in engagement time among Millennials according to comScore[17], while TrackMaven established that

[16] https://yougov.co.uk/ratings/technology/popularity/social-networks/all
[17] https://www.comscore.com/Insights/Infographics/Facebook-retains-Social-Media-crown-for-UK-Millennials

Instagram achieves the greatest engagement per follower[18].

But perhaps the real skill is not in deciding which one platform to use, but rather how to reposition your content to suit many different sites. You need to think how to target your audience successfully – from potential supporters to stakeholders and decision-makers – through the varied social media platforms by learning what you can about each one. For example, Twitter is conversational – best for sharing news and covering topics essential to your campaign; Facebook is similar but has an older audience. If you're trying to get teens involved, for example, they are leaving Facebook in droves; try Snapchat or Instagram instead (Instagram is the place to showcase images). The key is to find the platform that connects you with your target audience, and then tailor your post to the strengths of that platform.

Winning ways

To optimise your success on social media, try these tips:

- Post frequently – this helps to encourage engagement
- Use quality images – social media algorithms and users favour visually compelling content; use a photo editing app if necessary
- Collate – find information and images from other sources rather than just your own to provide variation and build community
- Make connections – social media is a two-way street and is a great opportunity to make valuable contacts

The hashtag

In Chapter 6, we touched on the importance of hashtags and how to choose one, profiling some great campaigns that have successfully built on their use. You should create a unique hashtag

---

[18] https://trackmaven.com/blog/instagram-analytics-ultimate-guide/

for your campaign as it offers another way for people to find, identify and share your work. Do your research and create an original phrase, because while they are predominantly used on Twitter and Instagram, they make your content viewable by anyone who has an interest in that topic, way beyond your followers. And the wider your audience reach, the higher your chances of success.

You can also use existing hashtags to piggyback on social media trends, opening up your posts to even more people. The homepage of Twitter shows the trending hashtags you could climb aboard, often including humorous ones that are having a moment and allow you to get your message across in a less serious way. Examples include #MySuperPower, #TwoThingsThatDontMix, #MisheardLyrics and #1LetterWrongMovie. There are also regularly occurring hashtags that you can plan ahead for – try to be as creative as you can with them. There's more than one for every day of the week:

- #MondayMotivation, #MancrushMonday, #MondayBlues
- #TipTuesday, #TravelTuesday, #TuesdayTruth
- #WomanCrushWednesday, #WednesdayWisdom, #WayBackWednesday
- #ThrowbackThursday, #ThursdayThoughts, #ThirstyThursday
- #FollowFriday, #FridayFact, #FlashBackFriday
- #SaturdaySwag, #Caturday, #SaturdayLove
- #SelfieSunday, #SundayFunday, #SundayMood

Charities and non-profits are also using 'social good hashtags' as a way to encourage engagement online. The tags include #volunteer (often used to show appreciation for top supporters), #donate, #dogood, #causes, #socialgood, #change and #changemakers.

Social media schedulers

It's likely you're running your campaign in your spare time, which is limited by other responsibilities, but social media needn't be as time-consuming as it first appears. There's an easy way to manage social media to avoid being overwhelmed and that's by using free versions of cross-platform social media schedulers like Hootsuite[19] and Buffer[20]. There are pros and cons of each, but they both perform publishing and scheduling well, and cover the main social media platforms.

Because it was designed as a social management tool, the analytics Hootsuite provides cover the content you post, how your social networks are performing and social traffic, while Buffer just gives feedback on the content you post from the platform itself. However, users report that Buffer is simple to use and intuitive. Of course, since they are free you can use both!

Other options include using Facebook's own in-app tool to schedule posts via its Groups and Pages – there's no time limit on how far forward you can work, which is a great plus point. Later.com, originally designed for Instagram but now also usable on Facebook, Twitter and Pinterest, also offers a free version that allows you to schedule your photo and video content on social media. You could try Planoly (for Instagram), Tailwind (for Pinterest and Instagram), Ripl and Recurpost.

But don't schedule all your social media posts as you risk losing natural engagement, and might miss the opportunity to make timely updates. Some algorithms also penalise third-party software use.

Going viral

According to the Urban Dictionary, something that 'goes viral' is an image, video or link that spreads rapidly through a population

---

[19] www.hootsuite.com
[20] www.buffer.com

by being frequently shared with a number of individuals. These days, for something to be considered to have gone viral, it will have to have had millions of views. Think of the original Baby Shark or the gymnast Katelyn Ohashi's Michael Jackson routine at the National Collegiate Athletic Association meet.

There have been some notable social campaigns that have attained viral status, but in most cases they have the power and finances of a business or some other large organisation behind them. These include the April 2013 'Real Beauty Sketches' campaign by Dove. It saw an artist sketching two portraits of the same woman; the first only by a description of the woman herself, the second based on how someone else described her. In each case, the women had given a far more negative outline than the stranger, and the campaign reached its aim to demonstrate 'You are more beautiful than you think'.

Another viral video was called 'Girls Going Wild'. Filmed in Amsterdam's red light district, dancers in shop windows performed a routine to delighted onlookers. As the dancing comes to an end, however, the crowd soon realises that the display is in fact highlighting forced labour, sexual slavery and commercial sexual exploitation. Stop the Traffik, a global movement aimed at putting an end to human trafficking, commissioned the performers.

Water charity Waterislife.com found viral success with its *First World Problems* film. It showed destitute Haitians reading tweets from the #FirstWorldProblems hashtag, which included postings such as 'I hate it when I have to write my maid a check [sic] but I forget her last name'. The video highlights the stark contrast in very simple terms by building on one of the Internet's most widespread memes, urging people to donate to help those who live in extreme poverty to have access to clean water.

Don't feed the trolls

A sad part of the Internet and social media is the existence of 'trolls' – individuals who use the medium to make unsolicited and/or controversial comments to provoke an emotional reaction or start a fight or an argument. Unfortunately, trolls delight in any controversy and will seek out social issues and political campaigns to post inflammatory and digressive messages. Celebrities like Stephen Fry, Graham Norton and Lily Allen have all left Twitter because of such unpleasant attention. Trolls thrive on attention, and so the best way to deal with them is simply to ignore them. Better still, if they are posting on a website or social media page or group for which you are an administrator, you can simply delete their comments or block them. Problem solved.

Case Study – Sarah Brisdion

Sarah Brisdion campaigns for disabled rights and fully accessible 'Changing Places' toilets in all large public venues and places. She is mother to twins, and her son has cerebral palsy. She is frequently faced with toilets that do not meet her son's continence needs. Changing Places toilets offer larger changing benches, hoists and larger floor space suitable for the children and adults who require them.

There are more than a quarter of a million people who need Changing Places loos, including those with learning disabilities, motor neurone disease, multiple sclerosis and cerebral palsy, as well as older people. Without accessible facilities, many people are forced to stay at home rather than risk visiting places where they cannot use the toilet – or use nappies and lie on toilet floors to change them.

Sarah has engineered several awareness

campaigns that have received lots of media attention. Designed to both shock and be humorous, Sarah's #LooAdvent campaign saw her post festive toilet selfies in the run up to Christmas 2017. In 2018, she sat on a toilet in London's Baker Street for six hours for her #PantsDown4Equality protest.

Sarah says her #LooAdvent campaign gained more press coverage than she could have hoped for. It featured on BBC TV and radio (her particular highlight was being on BBC Radio 2's *Jeremy Vine* show), Sky News and on Channel 4's *The Last Leg* with Adam Hills, Josh Widdicombe and Alex Brooker taking their own loo selfies in support. Bloggers also picked up the story.

The campaign resulted in new facilities being installed in several places, most notably in the Mayflower Theatre in Southampton. 'This is a huge breakthrough and makes the theatre the only venue where Changing Places users can see a big production or West End show,' says Sarah, adding, 'There are no theatres in London that offer these facilities.'

Throughout her campaigns, Sarah has used hashtags, which she believes helped to gain press coverage and to reach a wide demographic, including a younger audience. Sarah is a big fan of Twitter, because in her opinion it is 'fast-paced, easy to track and it was easier than other social media platforms to target celebrities and journos for the exposure I needed.' Sarah also uses Facebook, making the posts there longer and more detailed in order for them to make sense.

The involvement of key celebs was also critical to Sarah's campaigns. *The Last Leg*'s Adam Hills, comedian Sally Phillips and Sky Sports pundit and former footballer Matt Le Tissier all tweeted Sarah's

#LooAdvent images daily. They brought 'a combined reach of over a million followers that would probably never have seen the campaign,' says Sarah, adding, 'Tweeting them daily was easy and fast!'

Her final piece of advice to others considering a social media campaign to support their cause is to plan campaigns carefully and schedule posts in advance. 'I took photographs daily and wrote the post as I was making them ... A lot of stress could have been saved if I planned ahead,' she says, an approach she's going to adopt for her next campaign.

Takeaways

- Social media is the natural home for campaigns, offering relatively cheap and easy coverage with a wide reach
- Take time to learn about each platform and consider which ones you will concentrate on, tailoring your posts to fit
- Coverage on social and traditional media often overlaps and works to support each other
- Post on social media regularly, using schedulers to ease the load
- Encourage engagement and interaction, but block and ignore the trolls!
- Learn how hashtags can help raise your profile and bring more supporters to your cause

Blogging

In 2018, software recommendation platform Softwarefindr.com estimated that there were around 505 million blogs online. Indeed, practically everyone is familiar with the concept. What started as a way of keeping an online diary has mushroomed into a powerful online presence, one you perhaps don't want to miss out on.

Way back when

But the humble beginnings of what we see today date back to a 1994 college student and what he referred to as his personal homepage. By 1997, they were known as 'weblogs' and two years later just 'blogs', becoming the Merriam-Webster word of the year in 2004. In 1999, the platform that was to become Blogger was just getting started and went on to become responsible for taking the concept to the mainstream, by making it easy for anyone to publish a blog.

Why should I blog?

During the noughties, blogs experienced exponential growth, with the blogging platform WordPress launching in 2003. Within a few years, blogs were mainstream, with traditional media and other businesses creating their own official blogs. Soon microblogging took off and, in 2006, Twitter was launched, then Tumblr a year later. Development began to slow as blogs became widely accepted and an integral part of our online culture. As social media has grown, and video and podcasts have taken off, blogs have become just one part of an online presence.

As well as being an integral part of the way we communicate today, blogs build authority – writing one will help show people you know what you're talking about. If you run a website, too, using a blog can help drive traffic there. If you start a blog, publish useful content regularly to establish an audience and build engagement. Offer statements and statistics to help your cause – and share links on your other social media pages to keep potential new supporters and stakeholders interested. Spend some time deciding what you want to achieve with your blog – do you want people to sign a petition, change their behaviour, write to a local MP or meet up for an event? Are they looking for facts, for support, or other practical help?

What is an 'influencer'?

Increasingly, bloggers have become linked to the phenomenon of 'influencers' – particularly as some influencers will also have blogs alongside other social media accounts. An influencer is essentially an individual who has the power to affect decisions of others because of their authority, knowledge, position or relationship with their audience. Some of them have become a celebrity of sorts, often working within a particular niche.

However, as influencers became all the rage in marketing, a backlash occurred as their real worth was questioned. Many have been accused of buying audiences rather than growing them organically. In January 2019, hundreds of Instagram influencers were warned by the UK advertising watchdog, the ASA, because of a failure to disclose to followers when their content has been sponsored or paid for by a brand. In the wake of this, tougher rules covering social media are expected.

Another term that is associated with blogging and social media is 'online ambassador'. This describes an individual hired by an organisation to represent the brand in a positive light. A company might hire a celeb to be seen with their products, for example; fans of that celeb are therefore more likely to buy items endorsed by someone they admire or trust.

Many charities also employ this tactic – asking ambassadors to talk about their work or a social issue when they can. Ambassadors for the Prince's Trust include Caroline Flack, Holly Willoughby, Ant McPartlin and Claudia Winkleman. Everyday people often become fundraising ambassadors for charities they have personal experience with, inspiring people they know to become involved, attending events and generally helping to spread the word about the organisation.

The blogging community

Just because you set up a well-written and worthy blog, that doesn't mean your work is done. One of the harder aspects of blogging is managing to drive visitors (called 'traffic') to your blog. There are several ways to do this:

- Join blogging communities
- Comment on other posts on similar topics
- Offer to guest post on other blogs
- Linkys
- Use your own social media

Blogging communities are virtual social networks for bloggers. The idea is to make new contacts and share the workload of driving traffic to each other's blogs. With so many blogs in existence, it's likely you'll find a community of bloggers who share the same subject matter and ideals as you. They work on the basis that everyone puts the effort in – so if someone else shares or comments on your posts, you should return the favour. You might also choose to write about other bloggers – or include links to their posts in your writing – and vice versa.

Another option is to write for another blog – this is called guest posting. Bloggers ask for guest posts to cover periods when they know they will struggle to post, like when they go on holiday or other work is keeping them busy. Regular posting is key to maintaining your audience, so popular bloggers want to avoid any down periods.

The power of the link

Another option is to take part in a 'Linky' or 'Link Up'. One blogger will host a regular post that allows other bloggers to add their post on the topic to it. Those participating in the Linky visit the other posts and comment and help to share the blog across social media. Look out for these regular Linky options:

- BloggerClubUK
- Tried & Tested Tuesday
- #DreamTeam
- That Friday Linky
- Silent Sunday
- Read With Me

But why is it important to share links, comment, guest blog and link up? Because it creates 'backlinks' – which just means a link from another website to yours. Search engines like Google use links to find you. When someone links to your site, a search engine spider can crawl through that link, discover your site, and index (or make findable) your newly created content. Without backlinks, search engines can't find your content – and can't show web users it's there.

When you link to other pages with a good page rank (a way of measuring the importance of website pages) and domain authority (a search engine ranking score) your rating also goes up by association, meaning you'll appear higher up in search results.

Social media for bloggers

It's no surprise that bloggers are also active on social media – and one place to make your mark in the blogging arena, gaining more and more attention for your own blog, is by joining blogger-specific Facebook groups (try Official UK Bloggers) and by connecting on Twitter, where you can use #blogger to find new connections.

There are also blogger conferences and networking events out there in the real world. These include the Blogtacular conference and BlogCamp events.

First steps

So how do you build a blog? Thankfully, there are ready-made platforms to help you set up a blog quickly and for nothing (although you can pay to upgrade your blog – more on that later). A couple of options are listed below – it's worth playing with all the software first to see which you like, rather than chopping and changing along the way.

WordPress and Blogger

WordPress is an incredibly popular site among bloggers – and others looking for a way to create a website by themselves. With this type of tool, you don't need to know about coding or HTML as it provides templates that are customisable to some extent. If you opt to pay for certain elements, you can make your pages stand out from the free templates. When you use WordPress.com, your blog is hosted by WordPress and you won't need to buy a domain name or find a server to host your site, so your URL will end in wordpress.com.

If you're happy and able to pay, you can use WordPress.org, giving you full control over your blog's design and the option to get involved in some coding, and use plug-ins (little programs you add on to achieve certain functionality). You will have to buy or build your own template and find somewhere to host it. You can, of course, outsource the technical side of things, too, although if you're campaigning on a budget, it's unlikely you'll want to splash out.

Blogger is Google's free blogging platform, and it's incredibly easy to use. There are a variety of templates and your blog's URL will end in blogspot.com. You can also buy your own domain name and use that. It's not unusual for bloggers to start out with the simple Blogger platform and move to another – like WordPress – as they become more confident.

Other options include Medium and Tumblr, though the latter is really more of a social network than a blogging platform, and is often used for those with 'fandom' blogs.

Not for you?

If you're not sure whether a blog is right for your campaign – or you know realistically that you don't have the time or resources to make a good job of it – it still pays to be aware of the opportunities other people's blogs could offer. Working with bloggers is much like getting press coverage – another way to drum up support and influence people to make change. Bloggers often have targeted niche audiences, so you can offer to write a piece – or ask if you and your campaign can be featured. It's easy to get in touch via email or on social media, so go and introduce yourself, maintain the relationship and say thank you if you're featured.

Case Study – Kate Metcalf, Women's Environmental Network

The Women's Environmental Network (WEN) was founded in 1988 to offer a different way of thinking about and acting on environmental issues, using the perspectives and voices of women, which the group feels are often overlooked and undervalued in the environmental movement.

More than thirty years later, WEN still works to ensure more women lead conversations and become part of the decision-making process on environmental issues. WEN is the only UK charity working on issues that link women, health, equality and the environment.

One of WEN's most recent campaigns is the Environmenstrual initiative, which aims to make healthy and eco-friendly menstrual products affordable and available to all, and encourages women and people who menstruate to try #PlasticFreePeriods. The campaign offers workshops in schools and universities, runs an annual Week of Action in October and educates people to dispose of menstrual products in a more environmentally friendly way.

Co-Director Kate Metcalf explains that WEN decided to create a blog section on its website 'to engage more people around the issues that we care about and are working on', including its campaigns and grassroots project work in East London. WEN asks organisations that it collaborates with, as well as volunteers and interns, to write blog posts, which helps it to offer lots of different voices, increase the number of posts available and also to nurture and encourage confidence in those who are passionate about issues related to WEN's work.

Kate says the blog has been an effective tool in campaigning, helping WEN to reach out to different partners involved in its campaigns and to highlight specific issues that they are working on. They describe it as a 'two-way process'.

Inviting guest bloggers has also enabled WEN to bring in experts whose credentials further strengthen the campaigns. And while WEN links to academic reports and research, it also writes its own accessible posts for non-expert readers, meaning the blog becomes a 'key link between academics and experts', transferring the information to its supporters to increase awareness and equipping them to take action.

Kate says the blog has been fairly easy to manage, as it produced some guidelines that it sends to all contributors. She also says that each new post is shared on its own social media – and WEN will ask guest contributors to share the piece on their platforms to encourage take up. Her advice to those considering a campaign blog is to 'keep it simple and reach out to different people who can support your campaign'. She adds, 'Make sure you include lots of good photos on your website and don't make it too text heavy.'

She says it's good 'to also have a presence on Instagram, Twitter and Facebook if you can, as you can reach many people this way', and recommends having 'a simple YouTube video about your campaign' as another effective way to get your message across.

Takeaways

- Blogs are an increasingly popular way to have an online presence
- Use your blog to build authority, providing statements and statistics to help your cause
- Ask yourself what you want to achieve with your blog; do you have a call to action for example, such as a petition to sign?
- Consider asking supporters to write blog posts; this shares the workload and provides a variety of voices
- Blogs help you to reach out and engage with your audience, enabling you to pass on campaign news and details
- Remember to use social media to promote each new blog post
- Keep your blog posts easy to read, with lots of strong images to hold the reader's attention
- Increase your reach by becoming active in the blogging community and taking part in popular 'link ups'

15

Websites

When you're running a campaign and trying to push for change, you're usually short on both time and money. Organising meetings, protests and fundraising alongside contacting decision-makers, planning outreach and fundraising will probably take up most, if not all, of your time. You might ask yourself, 'Do I really need a website?' Ultimately, only you can decide whether a web presence is important to your activism, and if having one will bring you closer to your goal – or if your time is better spent elsewhere.

That said, a website offers the following advantages:

- It serves as an initial point of contact
- It allows you to put your opinion – and supporting material such as photographs, case studies and research – in one place for interested parties to view as and when they want
- It makes you appear professional
- It can help you find new supporters
- It can be a cheaper option than advertising and providing printed information to interested parties
- It offers global reach twenty-four hours a day

Where to get a free website

Some platforms offer basic websites for free, offering users paid-for upgrades that allow them access to more advanced features, personalised templates and their own domain name. If you're happy to stay in the free arena, however, you have several choices:

Wix.com

Over 110 million users in 190 countries use the cloud-based web development platform Wix to create a website. You don't need to code and it's straightforward to design the look you want using one of hundreds of templates. There's also a drag-and-drop editing tool and up to 500MB storage. If you want advanced features or your own domain name, then you can pay for an upgraded package.

Weebly

Website and eCommerce service Weebly also offers a very basic free website, with a drag-and-drop editing tool, SEO prompts, structured but customisable templates and up to 500MB storage.

SITE123

This website builder uses an editor system rather than a drag-and-drop tool and is quick and simple to use. It offers a choice of modifiable templates and up to 500MB storage with the free option.

WordPress.com

Yes, the popular blogging platform can also be used to build a website – but some argue that means it can be limiting in functionality. However, it has a solid reputation for built-in features inherited from its long history in the market. If you're already familiar with WordPress and want something basic, it could be a good option.

Making your website worthwhile

Just like having a blog, it's not enough to have a great looking site that is populated with brilliant content and technically perfect; you still have to make sure people can find you. Bear in mind, however, that ending up on the first page of a Google search is a fine art –

and companies are paying a fortune to professional geeks to ensure that they make it.

One way you can try to get higher up in search results on Google is by being aware of the practice of Search Engine Optimization (SEO) as you write your website copy. Google uses complex algorithms that scan every piece of every page it finds and judges how relevant the information is for a specific keyword. And sometimes Google changes the algorithms – just to keep everyone on their toes!

There are standard tips and tricks though – and these include the following:

- Use plenty of subheads
- Use key search terms within your headings and body copy
- Update content frequently
- Make sure you have links to other sites – and ideally links on other sites that direct traffic back to your site, too
- Ensure you are making your site accessible by adding clear descriptions for images to help the visually impaired, for example
- Make sure you've added descriptive titles and meta descriptions (the templates you follow should have a specific section for this)
- Get rid of duplicate content

Domain names and hosts

If your own website is central to your campaign and you are investing some money in it, you should also look into buying your own domain. The domain is the name that people will type into the search bar on their Internet browser – usually ending in '.com' or '.co.uk'. You can do this via a registrar such as Namecheap or Domainr. Some people choose to buy the same website name with various endings (like '.net') to ensure no one else nabs something confusingly similar or posts content that could be detrimental to your aims.

A host is a third party that handles where you'll 'keep' your website – your content will be stored on a server that is always connected to the Internet so that people can access your site. Simply put, a host 'hosts' your website on a server. Namecheap also offers hosting services as do Wix, Weebly (as part of their paid-for packages), GoDaddy and Bluehost.

Other tips

Remember to use your social media profiles to drive traffic to your website by cross-posting links to your pages regularly. Add your website address to any literature you produce and hand out, and put it on to your email signature, too. If a stand-alone website is beyond your reach at this point, a Facebook page or a blog can work just as well.

Case Study – Helen Diplock

Helen's second daughter Rosie has Down's Syndrome (DS), a genetic disorder also known as trisomy 21 because it is caused by the presence of all, or part of, a third copy of chromosome 21. Helen works as an advocate for people with Down's and also runs the T21 Allstars website, that both charts her story and shows T21 in a positive light using curated content from the DS community. The website also has a shopfront selling items that celebrate Down's.

Helen says having Rosie has been a positive experience that gave her a passion and drive she didn't have before she became her mother, despite being shocked at Rosie's initial diagnosis. While she knows there are 'many people with trisomy 21 who have a strong voice, and they need to speak for themselves, and we need to create that space, and listen to them', she also understands that not everyone with T21 has a voice; Helen provides that voice for her daughter and many others.

She began her advocacy with a website because she enjoys developing and designing them and because she wanted a medium that would enable her to have a blog, share stories of others with T21 and an online shopfront – she has collaborated with a jewellery company to design a necklace, part of the sales of which go to a Down's Syndrome charity that shares positive stories. She finds her website allows her to write longer, more thought-provoking pieces, because 'sometimes the complexity of Down's Syndrome cannot be captured in an Instagram or Facebook post'.

Helen's top tips for those thinking about starting a website to make a positive difference are: 'Just start it, and connect with others who have similar blogs and campaigns.' She has found the community of bloggers that post about Down's Syndrome really positive and supportive, and says, 'Find your tribe!'

Helen admits that at times her campaigns have been challenging – when her daughter is having a tough time medically it might be harder to post a blog, for example – but part of the message she wants to get across is the whole truth about what it's like to have a child with T21.

This is offset by the positive impact she has had with her work, particularly knowing her message is reaching people with high-probability diagnoses in pregnancy, new parents, midwives and priests; 'It's so rewarding to see their attitudes change,' she says. She's also proud of what she has achieved by working with her local NHS Trust to develop a pathway for children with Down's. For over two years, Helen has discussed the language used by medical professionals, working with them across the UK to share best practice. She knows she has made a difference for many local families, too, with monthly clinics for children with Down's Syndrome, a lead Nurse and a dedicated Consultant all now available.

And she's also incredibly proud of Rosie. 'She's the superstar behind it all. The joy of our lives, she just lights up every room she's in.'

Takeaways

- A website allows you to fully support a campaign, offering plenty of space to educate, fundraise and engage
- Free sites are available at Wix.com, Weebly, Site123 and WordPress
- You will need to use a registrar to buy a memorable domain name; try NameCheap or Domainr
- It's important that potential supporters can find your site; consider learning some basic SEO tricks
- Try to connect with those who have similar sites and campaigns, who can support you
- Drive traffic to your website at every opportunity, via social media and by having your url on printed literature, for example
- Websites can be time consuming, so decide if having one will bring you closer to achieving your goal, or if your time is best spent in other ways

Part III

Everything Else You Need to Know

16

Budgeting and Fundraising

Wouldn't it be nice if you could take a stand and it cost nothing to do so? That would open up political and social debates to everyone whatever their age or background, right? Well, as you probably know, the world is far from an ideal place, and keeping an active campaign going may mean you have to splash some cash. And it pays to be realistic about the costs you may incur from the outset.

How much?
Some of the costs of campaigning might be obvious, such as printing literature, travel charges and high-visibility outfits for a team of stewards marshalling a protest to keep everyone safe. And while individually these charges may be small, they soon mount up – particularly if your campaign lasts several years. In the USA, for example, the stationery supplies sector received a massive boost in advance of the women's marches that ran across the country.

There are also costs that you might not notice or expect: reams of paper and cartridges of ink from your home printer as you research and prepare agendas for meetings; cups of coffee and cakes while you speak to those whose stories can offer case studies and evidence to support your campaign; and prizes and gifts you donate to events designed to raise cash for your cause. Some costs are not quantifiable – your time and energy, for example.

And then there are the costs you might hope to avoid – particularly large ones, such as the need to seek legal representation. You might also consider the money that you have lost by protesting, perhaps because you sacrificed a work opportunity to attend, and the extra you have had to pay in order to boycott one shop or product and go elsewhere.

What is free?

Home-made banners are very effective; they show just how determined individuals are to make their point, and the papers often take notice of the most authentic and creative examples. Use what you already have at home to make yours – card, old sheets, garden canes as supports, children's craft items.

To some extent, the Internet and social media have drastically cut the cost of communication for activists; there's no more need for snail mail and a stamp to get a letter in the local newspaper or endless telephone calls in order to contact the local council. Getting coverage in the media can be free; online petitions can be created without a charge.

If you ask, you might also get local companies and individuals to donate what you need. Perhaps a print firm might decide to support you and offer to create some leaflets without charging you? In my experience, kind members of the public would often turn up with hot drinks and snacks at our regular protests – they might not want or be able to stand alongside us physically, but they do want to show their support.

How to budget

When you're running a campaign, it is important to be aware of what you are spending and how to budget. It's a really simple principle – you just need to know what you have coming in and what is going out so that you can determine whether you are spending more than you should. You might be happy to pay out of your own pocket, of course – that's entirely up to you.

To ensure transparency and in case you ever need to justify what you've spent, you need to keep accurate records. You can do this via a spreadsheet or a simple form, or even using an exercise book. Just make sure you regularly write down any monies that have come in and what you've spent. Keep all invoices and receipts properly organised and to hand. Keep on top of everything; don't let it slide. As a campaigner, people are often ready to criticise you, so you need to know and be able to prove you have everything in order. There are many free online budgeting tools and templates if you are stuck.

The need to fundraise

In order to be able to keep protesting you'll need to raise money to cover your costs. But don't worry – being a fundraiser is not as daunting as it sounds!

There are loads of ways to raise money to support a cause, from organising a singles dating night or swishing event (a clothes-swapping party) to putting on a treasure hunt or quiz in the local village hall. You might choose to take part in a sponsored event – a walk, a run, a ride or even a sponsored silence or head shave. No one idea is better than the other; it will depend entirely on the people you hope will donate their time and money and on what sort of events you feel most comfortable with.

You can also head online to fundraise via sites like JustGiving.com and VirginMoneyGiving, which operates as a not-for-profit and so allows more money to reach the cause. This is sometimes called 'crowdfunding' and can be used to raise funds for a personal cause, whether the cause is associated with a registered charity or not.

Here are some more fundraising ideas to consider:

- Run a silent auction
- An auction via your Facebook page/group
- Host a movie night
- Organise a casino night
- Have some car stickers or t-shirts printed and sell them at a profit
- Hold a fashion show
- Plan a hot chilli eating competition

- Go 'old skool' and rattle a tin – ask for donations
- Arrange a dog show
- Set up a steps challenge
- Start a fantasy football league

A registered charity

Although not an option for every campaigner and campaign because of issues such as size, resources and the aim of political campaigning, when you start to fundraise, you might also consider registering as a charity. It gives those donating confidence about where their money is going and gives you a defined status that may attract more support and respect. Charities can also obtain tax relief on income, capital gains, inheritance, corporation tax and stamp duty. Some companies and organisations will only donate to registered charities. But you must fulfil certain criteria to register as a charity.

In England and Wales, the Charities Act says that a 'charity' is an institution that is established for charitable purposes only; and is subject to the control of the High Court's charity law jurisdiction.

Charities are not owned by anybody. The charity is controlled and its assets held in trust by a board of trustees. Trustees are responsible in law for ensuring that charities are well run to deliver their charitable purposes for the public benefit as set out in their constitution.

The Charity Commission[21] is the Government department that acts as the regulator for all charities in England and Wales. You have to register your organisation with the Commission if you meet the legal definition for a charity and if you meet either of the following criteria:

- Your charity is based in England or Wales and has over

[21] https://www.gov.uk/government/organisations/charity-commission

£5,000 income each year
- Your charity is a 'charitable incorporated organisation' (CIO) – regardless of its income

A CIO is a newer legal format that allows charities limited liability without having to register as a limited company at Companies House. As a legal entity, a CIO can enter into contracts in its own right, and has trustees who will not have any liability for the debts of the CIO, in normal circumstances.

To set up a charity, visit www.gov.uk/set-up-a-charity.

Alternatives to a registered charity

If your organisation doesn't meet the definition of a charity but still helps the community, you might choose to set up a Community Interest Company (CIC) instead. This is a company that helps the public, but is not a charity. There are also rules on the gov.uk site that govern this type of organisation.

Another reason not to set up as a registered charity is if one covering your remit is already in existence. It makes no sense to compete for resources with a similar group when you could work together instead.

If you're setting up a small organisation like a sports club or a voluntary group and don't plan to make a profit, you can form an 'unincorporated association' instead of starting a business. Alternatively, some people choose to set up a 'social enterprise' if they want to create a business that has social, environmental or community-based objectives.

Another alternative to starting a charity is to set up a named fund or a trust, this enables you to raise money for a certain cause, without the time and effort of setting up and running a charity.

There are many alternatives to founding a registered charity if you want or need to formalise your campaign to go forward. The best place to start your research is on the gov.uk website

(Companies House is also on this portal) where you can find more information about the regulations that govern the many options.

Reasons not to register

There are some good reasons not to register as a charity even if you do intend to fundraise – not least the admin tasks and legal obligations you'll incur in following charity law and preparing and reporting accounts. Charities are also not allowed to do certain things, including political campaigning, which may present a problem if you want to bring change. Those involved in the charity will also have to prove that they have no conflicts of interests and do not benefit in any way (unless incidental, like travel expenses to a trustee meeting, for example). These are all time-consuming responsibilities that could potentially derail you from your initial aims.

Case Study – Charlie Beswick

Charlie's son Harry was born with a rare cranio-facial condition called Goldenhar syndrome, meaning one side of his face is missing an eye, an eye socket, an ear, a nostril and a fully formed jaw. He also has autism and is non-verbal. Harry has had more than twenty hospital procedures, including two to restructure his skull and build an eye socket.

In response to the thoughtless way people have reacted to Harry, including verbal and online abuse, as well as following, whispering, pointing and even crying, Charlie, who is a teacher, has set up a charity to help people learn how to interact with those who have facial disfigurements. Harry also has a twin brother, Oliver, who has seen how people can judge others without getting to know them first.

Charlie has written a book to help other parents and runs a blog at Our Altered Life to share her experiences. Her 'More Than a Face' charity offers workshops and assemblies to schools to help children understand facial disfigurement better, to encourage empathy and understanding, and to build a generation that is tolerant and accepting of differences. Before-and-after questionnaires from Charlie's presentations show that 100 per cent of students felt that they would be kinder to someone with a facial disfigurement after hearing her talk.

By raising money to fund her charity, Charlie can offer her assemblies free of charge to schools who otherwise wouldn't have the budget to afford them. The majority of children are merely curious about facial disfigurement, Charlie says, and she wants her work to have an impact on the people's perception of those with it. Charlie accepts that one day she will die and leave her son as a vulnerable adult without her, but she hopes that she also leaves behind a better understanding. To date, Charlie has worked with over 1,500 children and young people to make that happen.

Charlie says she decided to register as a charity for three reasons. The first was for transparency, explaining that 'I knew that being a registered charity means I am monitored by the Charity Commission. I liked that layer of credibility and that it (hopefully) gives people confidence that any funds raised are being used in the right way.' She also wanted people to completely trust her and felt a registered charity number ensured that. Finally, she believes that her charity status allows her to apply for certain grants and funds that only formal charities are eligible for. 'Credibility and the access to more funds were a big factor for me,' she says.

However, applying for charity registration presented Charlie with the massive challenge of raising an initial £5,000 – one that she relished and met. Alongside her presentations, she has also been able to arrange a family fun day to include those with facial disfigurements and consider how else she can help families affected by such issues.

Takeaways

- Be realistic about likely costs right from the start of your campaign
- Keeping accurate records of what money comes in and out will help you budget and remain trustworthy
- Fundraising can take many forms, could you hold an auction, a fashion show or a film night?
- Becoming a registered charity brings a campaign financial transparency and credibility, giving supporters the confidence to donate
- Not everyone needs to, or can, become a registered charity to raise funds, and there are lots of alternatives

17

The Law for Campaigners

If you're new to protesting and advocacy, you might wonder what laws you are protected by and which ones you must obey. Staying within the law will be a pivotal concern for those embarking on all forms of activism.

Of course, all laws are complex – and ultimately if you find yourself in legal trouble, you'll need an expert to help you. The information contained here is only a brief guide to some of the main laws you should be aware of and is in no way meant to replace legal advice.

Peaceful protests are a human right

The right to protest and the freedom of association is defined in Article 11 of the Human Rights Act, a UK law passed in 1998. The law is based on the articles of the European Convention on Human Rights and gives you the right to speak freely and join with others peacefully to express your views. It applies to protests, marches and demonstrations, counter-demonstrations, press conferences, public and private meetings and more, but it does not protect intentionally violent protests.

Article 11 protects those rights when public authorities either stop a demonstration going ahead, take steps in advance to disrupt a demonstration or store personal information on those taking part. The law prohibits the State from interfering with your right to protest because it disagrees with protesters' views, because it's likely to be inconvenient and cause a nuisance or because there might be tension and heated exchange between opposing groups. Instead, it is duty bound to take reasonable steps to enable you to protest and to protect participants in peaceful demonstrations from disruption by others.

The organisation Liberty successfully used the threat of legal action backed by the Human Rights Act when the Metropolitan Police refused to close London roads to allow the 2018 People's Walk for Wildlife[22]. Westminster Council had put march organiser Chris Packham in touch with a private company that would charge £40,000 to ensure road closures rather than facilitate the protest itself.

Anti-fracking protestors win appeal

The legal right to protest peacefully was bolstered in October 2018, when a court of appeal quashed the jail sentences of anti-fracking protestors who had been convicted a month earlier of causing a public nuisance after clambering on to the roofs of three lorries entering the Cuadrilla base in Lancashire[23]. The protestors were the first environmental activists to receive jail sentences for staging a protest in the UK since 1932, when ramblers organised a mass trespass in the Peak District.

The appeal was supported by human rights organisation Liberty and environmental campaign group Friends of the Earth – with supporters arguing that the original punishments set a dangerous precedent.

Protesting isn't stalking

The Protection from Harassment Act 1997 (PHA) was brought in to protect people from stalking, although it can be used against activists who are protesting against a 'group of people', such as a company. If your protest is peaceful, though, and any communication (a letter campaign, for example) is polite, then you cannot be deemed to be breaking the law.

[22] https://www.libertyhumanrights.org.uk/news/blog/everyone-has-right-protest-not-just-those-who-can-pay-it

[23] https://www.telegraph.co.uk/news/2018/10/17/anti-fracking-protesters-freed-prison-appeal-judges-rule-sentence/

Sections 3 and 3A of that Act do allow companies to gain injunctions against protestors to prevent actual or anticipated 'harassment'. This may restrict when and where you protest – and how many people gather.

New rules for London protests

The Serious Organised Crime and Police Act 2005 was brought into being to establish the Serious Organised Crime Agency and to control demonstrations in central London. It is controversial because it criminalises unauthorised demos within an exclusion zone of one kilometre around Parliament Square, and at the time was used to deal with anti-war campaigner Brian Haw, who lived for almost ten years in a peace camp there from 2001.

Under the law, anyone wishing to demonstrate outside Parliament must apply to the Commissioner of the Metropolitan Police six days in advance (or if this is not practical, then with no less than 24 hours' notice). The Act also applies to Trafalgar Square, Whitehall, Downing Street, Westminster Abbey, the Middlesex Guildhall, New Scotland Yard, the Home Office, County Hall, the Jubilee Gardens, St Thomas' Hospital and the London Eye.

The Act also created a new offence of trespassing on a 'designated' site. The site can be Crown land – land that belongs to the monarch or heir to the throne – or land a secretary of state believes is appropriate for designation in the interests of national security.

Anti-terror and activism

The Terrorism Act 2006, originally hailed as a response to the terror attacks of July 2005, has also become controversial for its use in response to protests. The Act created new offences related to terrorism and amended those that already existed, but recently the use of the law to convict fifteen anti-deportation activists drew criticism from the United Nations[24]. The campaigners cut through the perimeter fence at Stansted to prevent the deportation by the Home Office of sixty people from the UK to Nigeria, Ghana and Sierra Leone. The activists chained and locked themselves to the plane to prevent it being moved, claiming that to send the individuals to West Africa was an abuse of human rights and put the detainees at risk of further abuses. The authorities argued that the activists had put the safety of Stansted airport at risk. The group was convicted but spared a jail sentence[25]. At the time of writing, it was the first case that has seen terrorism-related charges brought against non-violent protesters in the UK and the activists were planning to appeal their sentences.

The 'Greenpeace 10'

Section 137 of the Highways Act 1980 prevents you from 'wilfully obstructing the free passage along a highway without lawful authority (as in permission from the authorities) or lawful excuse' (the Act allows for reasonable use of the highway in terms of such things as size of an obstruction, its location, the duration it is there, the purpose of the obstruction and if users of the highway are actually inconvenienced).

In 2017, ten Greenpeace anti-fracking protestors were charged under this section of the Act for obstructing the entrance to the Cuadrilla fracking site on the A583. The protest lasted just under eight hours and the group did not cover the whole of the entrance, with commercial vehicles able to exit. A District Judge threw out the case; the defence had argued that the group's actions were focused on Cuadrilla's vehicular access to the site and caused no disruption to the general public. They also argued that Articles 10 and 11 of the Human Rights Act afforded them 'lawful excuse'[26].

[24] https://www.ohchr.org/EN/NewsEvents/Pages/DisplayNews.aspx?NewsID=24141&LangID=E

[25] https://www.bbc.co.uk/news/uk-england-essex-47145449

[26] https://www.bbc.co.uk/news/uk-england-lancashire-41832800

Trespass and a Breach of the Peace

Trespass is a civil rather than a criminal offence. A civil case would be brought by a claimant who has the burden of proving that, more probably than not, the other party (the defendant) committed a civil wrong. Landowners, or their agents, can use reasonable force to remove trespassers, and police can assist in this if asked to do so. If you resist the police when they remove you, you may be arrested for obstructing a police officer. The police may also make an arrest to prevent a 'Breach of the Peace'.

A Breach of the Peace is violence or the threat of violence – and if your actions are likely to incite others to commit a violent act, then the police may arrest you to prevent it. You can be held until the threat of a Breach of the Peace has passed or you could be bound over to be of good behaviour by a magistrates' court. If the police direct you to do something to avoid a Breach of the Peace (such as asking you to leave) and you fail to comply, you could, in theory, be arrested for obstructing a police officer.

Aggravated trespass is a criminal offence; it covers trespass on land that intentionally disrupts a lawful activity, intimidates a person engaged in lawful activity or tries to deter them from carrying out that lawful activity. If convicted of aggravated trespass, you can be fined or imprisoned.

Other laws that could affect the manner in which you protest include wilful obstruction of the highway. The Highways Act 1980 (Section 137) defines wilful obstruction as: 'If a person, without lawful authority or excuse, in any way wilfully obstructs the free passage along a highway'. Another is 'Trespassory Assembly', an offence committed when a notice pursuant to Section 14 of the Public Order Act has been served on the organiser of an event and that person still goes ahead and organises the event, or when a person incites others to take part in the event, or when a person takes part in the event.

Organising events

Certain types of public procession events require that the organiser gives the police at least six days' notice prior to the event (unless it is not practical to do so).

These include:

- A procession that demonstrates support for, or opposition to, the views or actions of any person or body of persons
- A procession to publicise a cause or campaign
- A procession to mark or commemorate an event

The advance notice must specify the date and start time of the intended procession, the proposed route and the name and address of the organiser/s. Even if your event is not classed as a public procession, it might be prudent to contact your local police station.

It is also an offence to organise or take part in demonstrations in a designated area without permission from the Commissioner of the Metropolitan Police. As stated earlier, the full list of restricted London landmarks that require permission comprises: the Houses of Parliament, Trafalgar Square, Whitehall, Downing Street, Westminster Abbey, the Middlesex Guildhall, New Scotland Yard, the Home Office, County Hall, the Jubilee Gardens, St Thomas' Hospital and the London Eye.

Film and pictures

Filming and taking photographs in a public place is legal unless proven to have been for criminal or terrorist purposes. This means that you are allowed to film a protest held in a public place – and that includes police or security staff who may be present. Some public places may, however, ask you not to film – such as stately homes, museums, churches, shopping malls, railway stations and council/government buildings.

You can be pursued through the civil courts if you film on

private property or in another place where a person can reasonably expect to have privacy. Taking photographs of an individual without their consent is also a civil matter, and you could be open to civil proceedings if you take a photo that could be seen as defamatory.

It is an offence to elicit information (which includes images) about members of the armed forces, police officers or the intelligence services, which is likely to be useful to a person committing or preparing an act of terrorism, or publishes or communicates information of that kind. In this case, you don't need to be using the information for terrorism yourself, so you must be careful if you are likely to be using a camera or filming where counter-terrorism and intelligence operatives are present.

The police are not allowed to seize a camera unless they believe it contains evidence of an offence.

Collecting money

If you want to make a street collection by both inviting and accepting donations to fund your campaign, you need to obtain a permit from your local authority. However, it is not illegal to accept money if people offer it to you, as long as you don't invite it. Defining the concept of 'inviting' donations could be as simple as being in possession of a collecting tin.

Libel and slander

Defamation is defined as the communication of false information that harms reputation. Libel covers defamation that is permanent; for example, if it has been printed or broadcast. Slander covers transitory statements that are spoken, but not broadcast. In the UK, defamation is a civil action only. To claim defamation, it must be shown that the statement:

- Was made to someone other than the claimant

- Caused, or is likely to cause, serious harm to the reputation of the claimant
- May expose the claimant to contempt, disliking, hatred or ridicule
- May cause the claimant to be shunned by society or avoided by people
- Was clearly applicable to the claimant (even if the name was not used, but some other description – such as a job title – made it obvious who the statement referred to)

You can also be sued for defamation if you repeat another person's statement, so it's not enough simply to accept what someone else has said as fact without checking its accuracy. However, if something has been in the public domain for some time and no action has been taken, then that means it becomes much harder for anyone to claim defamation. Defamation law also applies online, so watch out if you share or comment on other people's social media posts; but if the statement uses a nickname that other people wouldn't recognise, then defamation cannot be proven. Libel does not extend to the dead.

Where can I go for help and advice?

UK legislation is available to view online at www.legislation.gov.uk. The home page offers a search facility and some quick links to recent legislation and that which has been most frequently accessed.

Liberty is an organisation that challenges injustice, defends freedom and campaigns to make sure everyone in the UK is treated fairly. The group is made up of campaigners, lawyers and policy experts who protect rights and challenge abuse of power. It provides information and advice to members of the public on human rights issues. You can view its website at www.libertyhumanrights.org.uk or call the advice line on 0845 123 2307/020 3145 0461.

Case Study – Mike Schwarz, Bindmans LLP

Bindman & Partners (now Bindmans LLP) was set up in 1974 by a leading human rights lawyer and, in the last four decades, has established a reputation for defending civil liberties and human rights. Bindmans' founding commitment – to fairness and to ensuring access to justice for all clients regardless of their means – remains at the heart of its cases. The firm regularly litigates in the highest UK courts, as well as the European Court of Justice and the European Court of Human Rights.

Mike Schwarz, Senior Consultant at Bindmans, practises in the area of criminal defence, human rights and protest law. He is also the co-author of a leading textbook on the topic, *The Law of Public Order and Protest* (Oxford University Press, March 2010), which provides an in-depth analysis of the law relating to public order and the right to protest, as well as procedure and evidential issues. Mike is well known for representing political activists and campaigners on issues as diverse as the environment, animal rights, peace/disarmament, race and social justice. He has a particular interest in citizens' freedom of expression and freedom of assembly under articles 10 and 11 of the European Convention on Human Rights (EHCR).

Mike advises peaceful, symbolic protesters to be aware of laws such as obstruction of the highway or aggravated trespass, and says the Public Order Act 1986 often affects those on marches and demonstrations. Those engaged in 'direct action' or covert activities, may be affected by criminal damage offences, while harassment laws under the Protection from Harassment Act 1997 may be applied to actions directed at businesses.

However, he says that some activities which lie outside the sphere of protest might be considered criminal offences, but they are not crimes if they are a furtherance of one's rights of expression (article 10 of the ECHR) or assembly (article 11 of the ECHR).

Always consult a lawyer if you are arrested or invited for a 'voluntary' interview following an incident, says Mike, adding that many activists suggest you use recognised law firms with experience of protest law, rather than the 'duty solicitor'. He also says some activists may benefit from seeking advice in advance of taking protest action, to decide the format they choose. He warns, however, that lawyers are limited in advising what criminal law implications may follow.

Consider online information or material you find in print as a 'starting point – not the end – of getting information about the criminal law, police powers, etc.', explains Mike, because, while much information is available, some may be inaccurate or out of date.

Takeaways

- The law surrounding activism can be complex; if you're having problems, look for a professional who specialises in civil liberties and human rights
- Article 11 of the Human Rights Act 1998 provides for the right to protest and the freedom of association
- The NGO Liberty offers advice and support to those facing difficulties
- The controversial 2005 Serious Organised Crime and Police Act means that there are now added restrictions on protests in central London
- If you are organising or attending an event, it pays to be aware of all the rules and regulations that might apply, and to plan ahead
- Don't blindly accept legal information you are told or read on- or offline, it may be inaccurate or out of date

18

Personal Safety

Perhaps one downside of campaigning is the fact that part of the role involves speaking up and being noticed. This can make an advocate for change uncomfortable, particularly if they are not used to being in the public eye. You might also have concerns that, by raising your profile, you are exposing your friends and family to the same scrutiny. But with the right approach you can make the most of your visibility without compromising your own safety – or that of those close to you.

What is and isn't acceptable?
Taking part in and attending protests and marches is a cornerstone of democracy. If you intend to organise or attend a demonstration, do your research and plan ahead to both make an impact and stay safe. Check and abide by the laws that apply to your protest – and learn about any organisations you are demonstrating with. Violence and the threat of violence are against the law, so it's important that you remain in control at all times. Don't waste your time and distract from the merits of your cause by inappropriately targeting the authorities or individuals or by damaging private property. You are always responsible for your own actions.

Of course, it's likely not everyone will agree with the stand you're making. You can reasonably expect some people to express their disagreement – and a minority of those people might choose to do so in ways that make you feel uncomfortable and threatened.

If someone uses threatening, abusive or insulting words or behaviour towards you, and you believe that they intend to cause you physical harm, it could be a crime under Section 4 of the Public Order Act 1986. If someone directs remarks and abuse with the intention of causing you alarm or distress, they could be charged with committing a Section 4A Public Order Offence.

Hate speech

Verbal abuse that is based on a person's colour, race, disability, nationality, ethnic or national origin, religion, gender identity or sexual orientation is defined as hate speech. It is a controversial area of law, because the lines between free speech and hate speech can be difficult to draw. However, the Public Order Act does cover hate speech, particularly if it leads to a crime or criminal behaviour.

Language that is deemed to incite 'racial and religious hatred' or 'hatred on the grounds of sexual orientation' and language that 'encourages terrorism' can be found to be illegal. Any criminal offence can be a hate crime if it is carried out because of hostility or prejudice based on disability, race, religion, transgender identity or sexual orientation.

Stay safe on demonstrations

Marches, protests and demonstrations are legitimate methods of campaigning and activism. However, it's worth planning ahead for your own safety and health. I recommend that you:

- Protest in numbers and never leave a demonstration alone
- Be wary of people asking for personal or private details when you protest; you wouldn't ordinarily offer up this information to strangers
- Refer any interested parties to a campaign website or specially created email address or mobile number
- Be prepared for weather changes and the time and distance you will cover; bring water, food, sun protection, warm/dry clothes as necessary
- Be aware of your location and route, and tell someone where you are going

- Take a fully charged mobile phone, but also a separate record of an emergency contact in case your battery is flat or you have no reception

Make the first move

When you organise a protest where police are present, it's worth appointing one person as a representative of the group. This will minimise disruption to the protest and show you are not there to cause trouble. If you find yourself running into problems with the police, Green & Black Cross (GBC) is an independent grassroots project that offers legal support for protestors. It runs a Protest Support Line on 07946 541 511.

Making the first move also works well with the media – a designated spokesperson can be ready with all the facts and figures you want to pass on, which will help deliver a clear message.

It's a far more comfortable feeling when you have proactively and politely approached others to manage or record the event.

Keeping records

If you're taking part in any form of direct action, using a video camera or the camera on a phone is a great way to prove if someone threatened or harmed you. It's worth taking some general footage, too, so that you can show the atmosphere before anything you're unhappy about took place. For example, a video can show that you were protesting peacefully at a safe distance from those opposing your views. For this reason, if someone comes to speak to you directly – either to learn more or to complain or argue – you should be ready to record the entire exchange. Read up about your right to film in the previous chapter and be mindful to obtain the permission of any other protestors shown on the film.

Before sharing photos and film you've taken, however, you might want to consider using tools, such as ObscuraCam (Android) or Skitch (iPhone), to blur images to protect the identity of others.

When you take a picture or make a video, your digital camera/phone will also attach information such as time and location that you might wish to keep private. Check your settings, or erase with ObscuraCam for Android or Koredoko for iPhone (which allows you to share without 'metadata'). If you own an iPhone, you can prevent your iPhone from automatically tagging your photos with your location by going into Settings > Privacy > Location Services > Camera > and make sure you choose 'Never' for the camera app location.

Harassment

The law defines harassment as behaviour that causes you distress or alarm, and it constitutes both a criminal offence and a civil action under the Protection from Harassment Act 1997. Legally, the Act requires that you must have experienced at least two incidents by the same person or group of people for the behaviour to be classed as harassment. If the police do not want to take action, you can still pursue someone you think is harassing you through the civil court process, and you may succeed in obtaining an order or injunction to prevent them from continuing that behaviour. If the harasser does not cease when an order or injunction is in place, it could then be a criminal offence.

Examples of harassment include:

- Unwanted phone calls, letters, emails or visits
- Online abuse and bullying
- Stalking
- Verbal abuse and threats
- Smashing windows or using dogs to frighten you

If you're being harassed and you feel you're in danger, you can contact the police. If you think you're being harassed because of your disability, race, religion, transgender identity or sexual orientation, you can report the harassment to the police as a hate incident or crime.

Online safety

If you want to protect your privacy online, you must take time to learn about how to secure your social media and digital communications. Each app and site offers privacy settings so that you can restrict who sees your posts. It's also a good idea to limit the amount of information you supply and google yourself to check what is visible. Disable location tagging on your smartphone and have separate passwords for each platform.

In Facebook, go to your 'Privacy' settings under 'Account Settings' and select 'Who can see my future posts?' and then opt for friends rather than public. You can also Review posts that friends tag you in before they appear on your timeline by going to the 'Timeline and Tagging' within 'Account Settings'. You can block people from adding content to your timeline by selecting 'Timeline and Tagging' under 'Account Settings'. At the very top, you will notice a section called 'Who can add things to my timeline?' You can customise this feature by selecting 'Friends' or 'Only Me'.

Within Twitter, you can choose to keep your tweets public or protect your tweets so that only followers can see them. Go to your 'Privacy and Safety' settings; in the tweet privacy section, check the box next to 'Protect my Tweets'. Click the 'Save' button at the bottom of the page. You will be prompted to enter your password to confirm the change. However, if a Twitter account is needed for campaigning, it's better to set up a separate one that you can set to public, keeping your own details secure. It's worth going to the settings and privacy section on your profile anyway to check through what data you are sharing.

Within Instagram, you can choose whether your account is public or private. When you set your posts to private, anyone who wants to see your posts, followers or following list will have to send you a follow request first. The platform's help centre is easily navigable from www.help.instagram.com/ with full privacy and settings instructions and information about how to block comments and followers.

You can stop people from harassing you on the Internet by 'blocking' them and/or reporting them for their behaviour. Make copies of any threatening online conversations, save emails or take screen shots. Use this evidence to show your Internet Service Provider or the police when you report them. Many sites have built in reporting and review tools; Facebook uses a drop-down arrow by content, while Twitter has a dedicated page to report problems (www.help.twitter.com/forms/abusiveuser). You can flag a YouTube video as inappropriate by clicking on the flag at the bottom right of the video.

Remember – always call the police if you feel you are in immediate danger. Dial 999 in an emergency – or 112 across Europe. If you are deaf, hard of hearing or have a speech impairment, a text phone is available on 18000.

For non-emergency calls, telephone 101 (or 18001 101 for the text phone service). You can find your local police force via www.police.uk.

Case Study – Aisha Ali-Khan

Aisha is the former aide of George Galloway, who paid damages and issued a court apology to her in 2016[27]. Aisha is also the co-organiser for the London Chapter of the global Women's March movement, and a successful activist for human rights and women's rights.

Her petition to demand the suspension of prominent Oxford professor Tariq Ramadan while he

[27] https://www.theguardian.com/politics/2016/jun/20/george-galloway-damages-assistant-aisha-ali-khan-dirty-tricks-claims

was being investigated for sexual offences in France garnered 12,000 signatures in just one weekend. The don denied the allegations but took a leave of absence from the university by mutual consent[28].

Aisha was also responsible for a petition to demand a law change to stop non-disclosure agreements being used to silence sexual harassment victims.

Aisha has been the victim of harassment and cyber-bullying because she has repeatedly taken a stand against those who use their position in society, wealth and the threat of legal action to silence their critics. She feels we are living in an era in which people are trying to shut down the freedom of expression. Aisha says while 'experience has taught me having an online presence is important but not at the expense of your mental health', she believes social media is still an amazing platform that has given a voice to many people who are not normally able to speak out.

If you are being harassed or bullied online, Aisha recommends that you take screenshots and record any type of evidence. If you find you are not being taken seriously, record your complaints in writing and aim to build up a tangible body of evidence. When you report an issue, take the name of the person you speak to. If you are speaking to the police, you should ask for the officer's badge number. Always ask for an email address to keep in contact and ask for that individual again when you follow up. But remember, it's often the case that the person you are complaining about may have a different version of events, which the police may believe. 'Temper

[28] https://womenunited1blog.wordpress.com/2017/11/07/tariq-ramadan-leaves-oxford-university-by-mutual-consent/
https://www.theguardian.com/world/2017/nov/07/oxford-university-places-tariq-ramadan-on-leave-amid-claims

your expectations,' she advises, as a lot of complaints do not reach a satisfactory conclusion.

She believes self-care is an important tool for activists, and values the support she receives from friends and some of her family. She says she is lucky to receive emotional support from fellow activists and is able to switch off when she's with those not involved in campaigning, too. She also recommends accepting that 'you can't change the world on your own', and that by teaming up with others who hold the same beliefs, you can lighten the load. Aisha also believes that since much of the stress from activism comes from dealing with people who don't agree with you, it pays not to fall out with people over your beliefs. She also advises having a clear objective to achieve, so that you are not fighting indefinitely without anything to measure your progress by.

For direct action, Aisha believes in strength in numbers, feeling that people take the women's rights marches more seriously because of the sheer number of protestors they attract. She also thinks it pays to be mindful that not everyone will agree with you – and that it makes sense to downplay your protest for your own safety if you are coming to or from a demo alone. When you are at a march, be sure you know the name and number of anyone you are responsible for, and who to call in an emergency. If there are 'legal watchers' – there to maintain order and be a point of contact if there are problems – get to know them. 'Plan for things to go wrong,' she says, so that you are prepared if they do.

Takeaways

- Be aware that raising your profile may cause you to be criticised
- Temper your use of social media for the good of your cause with the importance of looking after your own health and safety
- Plan ahead to stay safe before, during and after attending a protest
- Use the settings on social media to ensure personal privacy, and the block and delete functions to silence abuse
- Record any and all harassment on and offline to build up a tangible body of evidence should you need it
- Know whom you can rely on for emotional support when things get tough
- Contact the police if you are in immediate danger

Everyone's a critic

Despite the fact that at school our children are regularly taught to respect historical figures who stood up for what they believed in, modern-day activists are often criticised. While we applaud change-makers like Gandhi, Rosa Parks and Emmeline Pankhurst and admire those who challenged the status quo in more creative ways – such as poet Wilfred Owen and author George Orwell – there still exists a negative attitude towards the modern-day campaigner. And for those of us who are prepared to speak out, that means we will have to deal with detractors who are uneasy about our views, and who are even more uncomfortable about the fact that we're prepared to do something about them.

Dealing with criticism

If activism is new for you, it's likely this is the first time you have considered the negative connotations that can be attached to campaigning, and the manner in which other people may try to pigeonhole and censure you. But bear in mind that every person who is prepared to stick their neck out has to deal with others who do not support or agree with their opinions and actions. This applies in many areas of life other than campaigning, of course – think of a chief executive, politician or sports coach. Criticism as an activist is inevitable; it can be wearing over time, contributing to burn-out – and it can hurt, especially if it comes from people who might support you in other areas of life. The secret is to deal with criticism productively.

Handle it like a pro

Nobody likes being criticised, but how you handle it makes all the difference. Someone, somewhere, will find a reason to project their negativity on to you. Oft-quoted research by American social psychologist Roy Baumeister[29] shows that it's human nature to hold on to negative emotions more strongly and in more vivid detail than positive ones[30]. Baumeister and his team believe it takes about five positive events to make up for one negative event. Ouch!

The good news is that there are some techniques for dealing with criticism and negativity. The first is to build a support network around you – look to those people (in all likelihood your fellow campaigners) for care, acceptance, additional feedback, perspective and consolation.

Another positive way to deal with the haters is to use humour. Within our puppy-selling pet shop protest group an incident involving an abusive male was made light of as the individual was in fancy dress at the time, making the situation somewhat ridiculous with each re-telling. Destructive criticism in the form of a personal attack says more about the critic than you. A rational person does not resort to insults and hostility, and such jibes are not worthy of a response or reaction on your part. Why dignify irrelevant comments?

Focus on what matters

Nothing good can come from dwelling on criticism and negativity; instead, ignore the insults and focus on your campaign. You can't please everyone when you want to make change, so it's best to concentrate on moving your plans forward, rather than letting criticism distract you. If you do want to challenge critics, and you feel you might learn something from their gripes, ask for specific complaints. Don't trade insults; enquire with sincerity and perhaps the feedback might be constructive. But just remember Dale

[29] https://psychology.iresearchnet.com/social-psychology/social-cognition/bad-is-stronger-than-good
[30] https://research.vu.nl/en/publications/bad-is-stronger-than-good-2

Carnegie's words in his book *How to Win Friends and Influence People*: 'Any fool can criticise, complain, and condemn – and most fools do. But it takes character and self-control to be understanding and forgiving.'

The inner critic

It's easy to moan about the critics, the people who call out obscenities at you when you wave your banner or make catty comments on your Facebook page from behind their keyboards. But perhaps one of the worst critics you'll face is the one you see in the mirror every day. Yes – you! Silencing your own negativity is often the greatest challenge you'll face on the way to achieving your goals.

Everyone suffers from an internal voice that casts doubts and undermines accomplishments. While an inner critic can be helpful to recognise our weaker points and push ourselves to be better, the negative nag within us often goes overboard. If you feel your inner critic is preventing you from achieving more, remember it's impossible to achieve anything without failing at something – and your critical inner voice is not a reflection of reality.

Try these techniques to tame your inner critic:

- Consider how these thoughts sound in the second person; it's likely you'd never phrase them in the same way if you were talking to a loved one; treat yourself with the same respect
- Focus on your successes – pick a fight with your inner critic on this basis and argue with conviction
- Accept compliments and take responsibility for your achievements; each time you do this the inner critic will die down
- Remember – regret is worse than failure; ask yourself how would you feel if you did nothing

- Talk about how you feel to someone you respect; their perspective and saying these things out loud will help you challenge negativity

The further you go with your campaign and the more success you achieve with it, the more faith you will have in your abilities. You will also become connected to a supportive community of like-minded individuals who will bolster your confidence and confirm that you have what it takes to achieve your goals. Bear in mind, even the most accomplished activist suffers from self-doubt.

In 2014, Harry Potter actress Emma Watson made a speech on behalf of the United Nations. During her talk, she revealed that she had suffered from nerves and doubt beforehand, but told herself firmly, 'If not me, who? If not now, when?'

Imposter syndrome

It's not uncommon to find that the most successful of people – campaigners included – believe it is luck rather than ability that lies behind their successes, and that sooner or later a person or an event will expose them for the fraud they really are. This confidence-sapping mind trap is actually a recognised phenomenon known as imposter syndrome. The term originates from a 1978 body of work by Dr Pauline R. Clance and Dr Suzanne A. Imes. The two psychotherapists determined that the syndrome was particularly prevalent and intense among a select sample of high-achieving women.

While some anxiety is hardwired into us – as an evolutionary survival skill – culture also seems to have an impact. It seems to be a peculiarly British trait not to want to be seen as an arrogant bragger, for example. Many researchers agree that women[31] and

[31] www.paulineroseclance.com/pdf/ip_high_achieving_women.pdf

those from minority populations[32] also experience impostor syndrome more[33], due to cultural inequities. Our upbringing also often encourages us to fit in leading to us downplaying our abilities.

Beating it

If you spot imposter syndrome affecting your work as an activist, you've taken the first step towards showing it the door. Now you need to concentrate on reframing your negative emotions and listening to your better confidence-building instincts instead. Ask your tribe for support and learn to accept compliments for your achievements.

When the going gets tough

Interestingly, the hardest of times actually allow us to succeed – as long as we don't shy away from the obstacles in front of us. In this way, criticism both from others or yourself can actually spur you on in your desire to make change.

Farrah Storr, the author of *The Discomfort Zone*, explains why it's essential to push your boundaries and challenge yourself in order to achieve your best. She draws on her experience when taking on the launch of *Women's Health* magazine with a low budget and a small team in uncertain economic times. She explains that it was when she regularly had to step outside her comfort zone that she was able to fulfil her potential and achieve what was later hailed as 'the most successful women's magazine launch of the decade'. Storr went on to revolutionise *Cosmopolitan* magazine, and as Editor-in-Chief chose plus-size model and body-positivity advocate Tess Holliday for the front cover, receiving both criticism and praise for her decision.

---

[32] https://www.insidehighered.com/news/2017/04/06/study-shows-impostor-syndromes-effect-minority-students-mental-health
[33] https://slate.com/business/2016/04/is-impostor-syndrome-real-and-does-it-affect-women-more-than-men.html

Storr's approach to life – facing discomfort head on in an attempt to unlock the potential you were unaware you had – accurately portrays how many activists discover new strengths and skills during their campaigns. Once you have learnt to deal successfully with both critics and your own self-doubt, you will emerge bolder and braver, and ready to bring about change.

Case Study – Jake Graf

Jake Graf is a writer, actor, director and transgender advocate. His own films include *X-WHY*, *Brace*, *Chance* and *Dusk*. Jake also appeared in the biopic film *Colette*, opposite Keira Knightley, and in *The Danish Girl*. His aim through his work has always been to give the trans and gender diverse a voice, a face, and to make marginalised groups know that they are seen and that they matter.

Jake is married to Hannah Winterbourne, an engineer with the British Army and the highest-ranking transgender officer. The couple are both patrons of Mermaids, an organisation that offers information and support to thousands of trans and gender diverse children and young people, and their families.

While Jake's work has been well-received because his films 'have resonated globally with audiences that had rarely before seen themselves on screen', he admits that 'as with anything that is available in the public sphere, there is criticism and the inevitable trolling', which he admits can do 'substantial damage'. However, he is pragmatic – accepting that such people are usually lonely and unhappy, with little better to do.

The trick, says Jake, is to ignore the online critics, who exist because 'those who feel they are overlooked or silenced can voice that dissatisfaction online with little fear of repercussion' and says he almost never engages, adding 'you usually won't change their mind, and it's quite frankly a waste of your own positive energy!'

Jake does find that when he and Hannah speak at a Mermaids event or at youth conferences, however, the issue of dealing with critics 'sadly comes up a lot', which is 'indicative of the level of this problem amongst our youth in particular'. He advises above all to keep in mind your own safety, saying, 'Very little is worth putting your own life in grave danger for' – and recommends 'a simple "delete and block" approach. As so many of our interactions are online nowadays, this is usually the most effective of options!' He also suggests you 'try and remember that the bullies and critics are much more miserable than you, and while those barbs or insults still hurt, you can simply switch off your computer or block them on your phone. They will always be angry, hateful people.'

Despite writing eight award-winning films and releasing his first feature-length film, even Jake still suffers from self-doubt. He attributes this to growing up in 1980s London, where 'there were no visible transgender role models at all, no representations [of transgender people] in the media or in films or books, which made for a very lonely and isolating experience'; he says that he had 'a childhood where I felt very much like there was something wrong with me, and that I didn't belong anywhere'. That feeling of uncertainty during his formative years has stayed with him, which often means that despite his personal and professional success, he often feels that 'this life is someone else's'.

Jake deals with these feelings head on 'by

remembering that we all deserve to be happy, and that if you work hard, try and be as positive and kind as possible – which is not always easy! – that you deserve to be here just as much as the next person.'

Takeaways

- Expect people to disagree with you, but choose to deal with criticism productively
- Don't waste time and energy on haters; focus instead on your campaign
- Even the most successful people suffer from self-doubt; the trick is to remind yourself that you deserve as much respect and kindness as anyone else
- Accept compliments and take ownership of your achievements
- Pushing your boundaries may be uncomfortable, but it's often the path to success

20

Am I Finished?

Within all activist campaigns there are various levels of success and failure. You should prepare to face both, and also a mix of the two. While you may achieve all or some of the goals you set yourself, you may fail with others. As the campaign progresses, new supporters and external factors change, new goals may be set, replacing your initial targets. In fact, one of the main reasons that I suggested you identify and set clear goals at the beginning of the book was so that you would be able to use these objectives to measure your progress further down the line. Lasting and real change is rarely effected overnight; many, many campaigns will continue for years before their impact is noticed and quantifiable.

How do I know if I won?
Depending on what you set out to achieve, your end point may be very obvious and tangible; for example, the release of someone wrongly imprisoned, the creation of a new law, a Government inquiry or compensation for those affected by your cause. If you reach this point, you can be assured you have done well, and be justifiably proud of your work.

However, some success will be harder to measure, making it difficult to see or understand your impact. This can affect your motivation to continue. One way to track your effectiveness is to monitor how much attention your issue receives from individuals and organisations such as the press, policy-makers, non-governmental and community-based groups. Consider tracking your campaign slogan, hashtag or main issue by setting up Google Alerts and using RSS Readers (such as NetVibes, Feedly or Reeder), which can aggregate the content published on the sites you choose to follow. You can also monitor Twitter activity by using keyword searches or mentions and tools on Hootsuite or TweetDeck.

Alternatively, you may need to look for research and statistics that cover the result you hoped to see, such as a reduction in knife crime, an uptake of a particular service that helps the homeless, less litter or more people cycling to work.

Case Study – Geraint Ashcroft

In 2014, teacher Geraint Ashcroft was diagnosed with cancer. Following two major operations that cured the disease but left him in considerable pain, Geraint retired through ill health and found himself at a loose end. Sorting through the recycling one day, and checking his local council's site, he was shocked to see that crisp packets couldn't be recycled. Research led him to the company TerraCycle, which offers free-to-use recycling collection schemes, funded by brands, manufacturers and retailers that are prepared to help.

In October 2017, Geraint decided to create a petition aimed at crisp manufacturers. As they are the largest and best-known in the UK, he asked Walkers to use recyclable, compostable or biodegradable packaging (although the emphasis later changed to the use of true biodegradable packaging). While initially the petition struggled to gain momentum, the media ran a story about thirty-year-old packaging being found, and petition site 38 Degrees offered to help promote Geraint's campaign. By August 2018, the petition had reached 300,000 signatures and Walkers' parent company PepsiCo invited Geraint and 38 Degrees staff to a meeting.

Geraint asked the company to commit to

biodegradable packaging as soon as possible, earlier than their 2025 target, to create a recycling system to reduce pollution in the interim and provide financial help for the voluntary organisations who were cleaning up its packaging. Walkers promised a press release within six weeks.

When that deadline came and went without a press release, Geraint put into practice the suggestion by 38 Degrees to recommend supporters posted back their empty crisp packets to Walkers. The Post Office publicly announced it was struggling with the packets, providing more publicity, and Walkers quickly announced a partnership with TerraCycle. The announcement came on Friday, 5 October, which was the day BBC's *One Show* was airing a piece about the campaign.

There are now over 8,000 locations where the public can drop off any brand of crisp packet to be recycled by TerraCycle. Geraint's campaign was successful and is making a massive difference to the amount of refuse that goes to landfill.

Geraint puts his success down to factors that were both planned and coincidental. The combination of involvement from 38 Degrees, media interest and the press coverage of the old packaging story contributed to create 'a perfect storm' he says. The feeling on hearing the announcement was one of 'pure elation' – not least because the scheme extended to brands other than Walkers and offered generous incentives to collectors, too.

Geraint admits his year of hard work had, at times, left him despondent, and that the announcement, while a tremendous achievement, was in some ways just the start. The next job was to push PepsiCo to help with another of his objectives – to clean up crisp packet litter. The company is now sponsoring beach clean-up events. Geraint also continues to push for the replacement of plastic packaging with a new biodegradable alternative, and was disappointed not to get other brands such as KP, Tayto and Seabrook to join in with supporting the Walkers scheme in a single collaboration. While KP has its own scheme, which suffers from fewer collection points and a smaller incentive, Tayto has reassured Geraint its scheme is already active in Northern Ireland and will be extended to the mainland soon. Seabrook, however, has said it will not be implementing any scheme.

Geraint has achieved so much in this, his first campaign, but he's not finished. He continues to campaign for a true solution from all crisp manufacturers (i.e. biodegradable packaging that breaks down into natural elements, in the shortest possible time), far sooner than the 2025 date that companies are currently working towards. I think the earth needs more Geraints!

Takeaways

- From the outset of your campaign, have a clear idea of what success will look like
- Expect some of your goals to change, and for new ones to be set
- Success can be hard to define and your results may not be tangible; ask yourself how you can measure your achievements
- Avoid burnout and take some time out, knowing you can return to your campaign at any time
- Own your achievements – be loud and proud!

You did it!

If you achieved one or all of your goals, it's important to own your success. This is to ensure that the changes you sought to effect are known about more widely – and do actually happen. Being bold about your achievements will also spur on others to push harder for other changes.

Make sure the press covers your victory. Often policy-makers reach an agreement to appease activists, but that might not translate into actual change unless the promise to do so has been well documented. You'll likely still have some work to do to ensure timely implementation goes ahead, so be prepared to keep on top of the issue and make some noise if the agreement is quietly pushed aside once the attention of the public drifts.

What if I failed?

Not all campaigns end in success, but all campaigns *do* have some successes along the way. At the start of a campaign, there is often a lot of interest and energy but, as time goes on, that wanes and your supporters may become distracted by things happening in their personal lives, they might move on or factions within the group may appear. It's important to keep motivation levels up and develop new tactics to bring you closer to victory. Recognise that plateaus and backsliding are part of the process.

Try not to be disillusioned if your work seems to stall; consider whether amalgamating with new, bigger groups can take your campaign further and focus on the potential outcome a more powerful alliance could have – even if you are no longer in the driving seat. Remember why you started out in the first place, and remind yourself of the individuals you want to help.

It can be hard to stay optimistic, so ensure you acknowledge and celebrate small positive steps – every single milestone you reached along the way could not have been achieved without you. Think, too, about what you have gained – new skills, confidence, friends and experiences. I can honestly say I never expected to go to a garden party at 10 Downing Street!

Avoid burnout

Organising and participating in social campaigns can be emotionally and physically draining – and even successful and experienced activists need to rest. If you're feeling exhausted by your advocacy, it could well be time to take stock and decide if you should move on and reassess your goals to avoid burnout. Share your feelings with your community, spend some time doing the things that re-energise you and take a break. This will help you to re-commit when you have more time, energy and resources. Try not to feel guilty if you need some time to look after your own needs – or if you feel it's time to change course.

Rediscover the things that motivate and drive you – and remember that change is possible. You've now built a dedicated group of skilled and engaged campaigners and, in time, the compassion that spurred you on in the first place will return and you'll be ready to start afresh and move on to your next challenge.

Additional Resources

Chapter 1

- Learn more about the #PeoplesVote marches, sign up and volunteer: https://www.peoples-vote.uk/march
- Get involved in the demand for real climate action: https://riseforclimate.org
- View the TEDx Talk by sixteen-year-old Greta Thunberg, the Swedish schoolgirl who started the school strike movement: https://youtu.be/EAmmUIEsN9A
- *This Changes Everything: Capitalism vs. the Climate,* Naomi Klein

Chapter 2

- Find out about government services: https://www.gov.uk
- What is local government? The Local Government Association explains the basics: https://www.local.gov.uk/about/what-local-government
- Natasha Devon's Mental Health Media Charter: https://www.natashadevon.com/the-mental-health-media-charter

Chapter 3

- For more information about GDPR legislation, visit: https://www.gov.uk/data-protection; https://ico.org.uk/for-organisations/guide-to-data-protection/guide-to-the-general-data-protection-regulation-gdpr/
- More about Claire Wright: www.claire-wright.org

Chapter 4

- National Council for Voluntary Organisations – offers advice and support for voluntary organisations: https://www.ncvo.org.uk
- Organise: https://www.organise.org.uk

Chapter 5

- The Chartered Trading Standards Institute: https://www.tradingstandards.uk
- The Information Commissioner's Office: https://ico.org.uk
- How to make an FOI request: https://www.gov.uk/make-a-freedom-of-information-request
- Hugo's Earthquake: https://hugosugg.wordpress.com

Chapter 6

- Melissa Mead MBE on Twitter @AMotherWithout
- The UK Sepsis Trust: https://sepsistrust.org

Chapter 7

- Canva is a free tool that allows you to create graphic designs – suitable for everything from social media posts to brochures. It also offers some free advice on PR: https://www.canva.com/learn/complete-guide-pr/
- Muckrack lists the portfolios of journalists – ideal to target those interested in your cause, and it also offers some free advice: https://muckrack.com/blog/2017/09/25/how-to-craft-a-winning-pr-pitch
- ResponseSource runs a media contacts database and a journalist enquiry service. There's a free trial that could prove helpful for activists on a budget: https://www.responsesource.com/
- Natalie Trice PR School on Twitter @natalietrice
- *Writing a Press Release – An Art, Not Rocket Science* by

Natalie Trice (Kindle Edition available on Amazon)

Chapter 8
- For all things crime and policing in England, Wales and Northern Ireland: https://www.police.uk
- Applying for a licence to protest in London: https://www.cityoflondon.police.uk/advice-and-support/organising-events/Pages/default.aspx
- Green & Black Cross – an independent grassroots project set up in the spirit of mutual aid to support social and environmental struggles within the UK: https://greenandblackcross.org

Chapter 9
- Change.org: www.Change.org
- 38Degrees: www.38Degrees.org.uk
- UK Government and Parliament Petitions: https://petition.parliament.uk

Chapter 10
- Amnesty: https://www.amnesty.org.uk
- Greenpeace: https://www.greenpeace.org.uk
- The Electoral Reform Society: https://www.electoral-reform.org.uk
- Campaign for Nuclear Disarmament: https://cnduk.org
- Friends of the Earth: https://friendsoftheearth.uk
- The London Cycling Campaign: https://lcc.org.uk
- Action on Smoking and Health: https://ash.org.uk/home/
- The Fawcett Society – the UK's leading charity campaigning for gender equality and women's rights: https://www.fawcettsociety.org.uk

Chapter 11

- APDAWG: https://apdawg.co.uk
- The APPG register and rules from Parliament: https://www.parliament.uk/about/mps-and-lords/members/apg/
- The APPG portal: https://www.appgs.org

Chapter 12

- Talk to the Press – a great way to get a story some coverage: https://www.talktothepress.co.uk
- Sell My Story – another news agency that could get you coverage: https://www.sellmystory.co.uk
- Hold the Front Page – a listing of UK press: https://www.holdthefrontpage.co.uk/
- Local Media Works – a list of regional press: www.localmediauk.org
- Media Info – a database of UK media contacts: https://media.info/uk

Chapter 13

- The beginner's guide to social media by software services company Moz: https://moz.com/beginners-guide-to-social-media
- Changing Places toilets: www.changing-places.org
- Sarah Brisdion on Twitter @SazBrisdion

Chapter 14

- The beginner's guide to blogging by Moz: https://moz.com/beginners-guide-to-social-media/blogging
- A directory of UK lifestyle bloggers – great for inspiration: https://www.hibs100.co.uk
- The Women's Environmental Network: https://www.wen.org.uk

Chapter 15
- For domain names and website hosting try: www.123-reg.co.uk, www.fasthosts.co.uk
  https://www.namecheap.com or https://uk.godaddy.com
- Trisomy 21 Allstars: https://t21allstars.com

Chapter 16
- The Institute of Fundraising: https://www.institute-of-fundraising.org.uk/guidance/
- The Fundraising Regulator, an independent, non-statutory body that regulates fundraising across the charitable sector in England, Wales and Northern Ireland: www.fundraisingregulator.org.uk
- Many of the large charities will have online resources for fundraising ideas and inspiration – try Kidney Research (https://www.kidneyresearchuk.org) and Cancer Research UK (https://www.cancerresearchuk.org/)
- Our Altered Life: https://www.ouralteredlife.com

Chapter 17
- Bindmans LLP: https://www.bindmans.com
- Other campaign groups also offer online advice for activists, try: www.animalrightsuk.org and www.network23.org/freebeagles

Chapter 18
- The Citizens Advice Bureau website has a dedicated section on finding legal advice: https://www.citizensadvice.org.uk
- Netpol seeks to monitor public order, protest and street policing, and to challenge and resist policing which is excessive, discriminatory or threatens civil rights: https://netpol.org

Chapter 19

- How to stand up to your inner critic – Rick Hanson, Forrest Hanson (IDEAS. TED. COM)
- The Discomfort Zone: How to Get What You Want by Living Fearlessly – Farrah Storr: https://ideas.ted.com/how-to-stand-up-to-your-inner-critic/
- Mermaids – supporting gender variant and transgender children, young people and their families: https://mermaidsuk.org.uk/

Chapter 20

- Look after your mental health by accessing support for stress and wellbeing from these organisations: https://www.mentalhealth.org.uk, https://www.mind.org.uk, https://www.nhs.uk
- TerraCycle UK – find a local recycling scheme: https://www.terracycle.co.uk/

Acknowledgements

I passed a portion of my misspent youth caterwauling along to Billy Bragg's 'There Is Power in a Union'. While I wasn't about to head off to become a shop steward in the coal industry, it left me with a respect for the strength gained from the support of others. Accordingly, this book couldn't exist without a coalition of collaborators, not least Tom Asker who took my pitch to an initial meeting at Little, Brown.

I also want to thank Julie, Ann, Marina, Yonni, Marnie, Jacqui, Niki, Emma and Kim – and everyone else who stood on a certain section of the A4 making a difference to the breeding parents held in puppy farms both here and abroad. Thank you, too, to the teams at CARIAD, ChancePixies, PupAid and BoycottDogs4Us who worked towards the same goal, giving us small cogs greater traction.

The book also wouldn't have been possible without those who spoke to me about their campaigns: Jo Kent, Sam Mastermann, Juliette Mann, Anna Turns, Caroline Giles, Natasha Devon OBE, Claire Wright, Usman Mohammed of Organise, Hugo Sugg, Melissa Mead MBE, Natalie Trice, Emily Lawrence, Rebecca Atkinson, Niall Couper of Amnesty, Dr Lisa Cameron, Marc Abraham BVM&S MRCVS, Sarah Brisdion, Kate Metcalf of WEN, Helen Diplock, Charlie Beswick, Mike Schwarz of Bindmans LLP, Aisha Ali-Khan, Jake Graf and Geraint Ashcroft.

Thank you, too, to Lorraine Platt who wrote my Foreword; she is a tireless and award-winning campaigner for animal rights, protecting wildlife through groups such as Blue Badger, Blue Fox, Blue Hare, Save the Asian Elephants and the Conservative Animal Welfare Association.

And then there's the support team at home – helping out with lifts to swimming and dance and desperate pleas for printer ink – as well as KEEPING QUIET when I'm tapping at the keyboard. Thank you to my family, my friends, my girls and, last but never least, my husband (who hates Billy Bragg and my singing of it in equal measure!)

Index